1,001
WAYS TO
Get Promoted

By
David E. Rye

CAREER PRESS

Franklin Lakes, NJ

1,001 WAYS TO GET PROMOTED
Cover design by Rob Johnson Design
Printed in the U.S.A. by Book-mart Press

To order this title, please call toll-free 1-800-CAREER-1 (NJ and Canada: 201-848-0310) to order using VISA or MasterCard, or for further information on books from Career Press.

The Career Press, Inc., 3 Tice Road, PO Box 687, Franklin Lakes, NJ 07417

Library of Congress Cataloging-in-Publication Data

Rye, David E.
   1,001 ways to get promoted / David E. Rye.
    p. cm.
  Includes index.
  ISBN 1-56414-430-5 (pbk.)
  1. Career development. 2. Success in business. I. Title. II.
Title: One thousand one ways to get promoted
  HF5381.R84 1999
  650.1--dc21   99-30192
                                                            CIP

Contents

Chapter 3: Selling Yourself   79

Chapter 4: Motivating Yourself   109

Preface

Whatever business you're in, your success depends on how well you promote yourself because no one else can do it for you. *1,001 Ways to Get Promoted* shows anyone, from non-managers to executives how to promote themselves by making dynamite presentations, networking a crowd, developing winning project teams, and hundreds of other self-promotional techniques that will catapult your career onto the fast track. And it is done in one concise, how-to reference book that's both fun to read and filled with hundreds of true-life stories that cover all of the critical promotional functions including:

✓ Organizing everything you do for success.

✓ Selling your ideas to get ahead.

✓ Motivating everyone, including yourself.

✓ Communicating with power and influence.

✓ Networking to develop strategic contacts.

✓ Teaming with winners to promote your ideas.

✓ Managing your way through any roadblocks.

In this results-oriented book, I'll tell you everything you need to know about get promoted. I'll show you all the mistakes to avoid, in a business-case environment, where you can relate directly to all of the promotional strategies covered. You'll be introduced to a wide variety of challenging situations where you'll have the opportunity to walk through logical approaches that you can use to get yourself promoted.

The Challenge of Promoting Yourself

What does it mean to promote yourself? Is the promotion game worth spending your energy on? Employees often get locked into playing the corporate game where someone else sets the speed of the treadmill and dictates how fast to run. Conversely, playing the promotional game can be a lot of fun because you control the speed of the treadmill and determine what promotional plays to use to move yourself up the corporate ladder. If you play the game right, you'll come out a winner and get promoted along the way.

Let's face it, business is a game where power and influence are required to get ahead. The object of the game is simple enough: Determine where you want to be on the corporate ladder, and then try to get there! Some people play the game for money, some for job security, others for recognition or personal objectives. When you play the promotion game, you will need to make rapid, complex moves if you want to win.

To successfully play the promotion game, you must first learn how the game is played and what techniques or strategies it takes to win. Your challenge along the way will be to refine your moves to a fine, cutting edge. Here's how the game is played: There are seven essential promotional tenets that you must learn to master in order to win. Like rungs in the ladder, once you have mastered one, you move up the ladder to the next rung. Although each tenet is autonomous and distinct from the others, they all interact to form a cohesive, interactive strategy that, if properly employed, will catapult you up to the top of the ladder, where you will meet or exceed your most ambitious promotional dream.

The Corporate Ladder

Managing

Teaming

Networking

Communicating

Motivating

Selling

Organizing

If the tenets are properly employed, they will help you significantly expand your sphere of influence and get you promoted. As the old adage goes: "It's not what you know, it's who you know." This is still partly true today. However, with the revamp of the corporate structure that has taken place in this country over the past decade and the renewed emphasis on productivity, the "who you know" slogan has been modified: It's *what* you know followed by *who* you know. The "who you know" must first believe in your capabilities before he or she will help you. Your ability to consistently demonstrate that you know what you are doing cannot be overemphasized. The illustration on the next pages shows you how the seven tenets interact with your sphere of influence, or the "who you know" in your world.

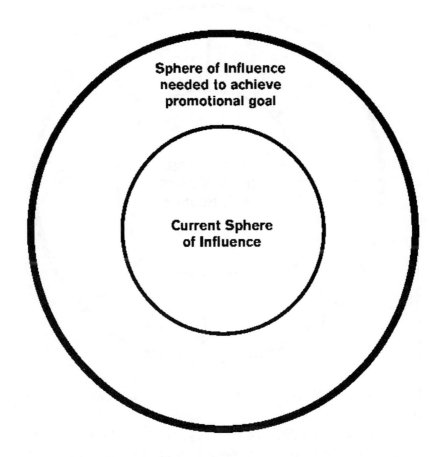

The outer sphere in the illustration represents your goal line, the top of the ladder, or where you want to go to achieve the promotional level you're driving for. It'll change as you become more proficient at playing the promotion game. The smaller inner circle represents where you are today, relative to the current level of influence you have within your organization. As you begin to expand your level of organizational influence, the inner sphere expands as well, until it ultimately touches the boundary of the outer sphere, and you will have achieved your promotional goal. The illustration on the next page shows what you need to do to expand the inner sphere.

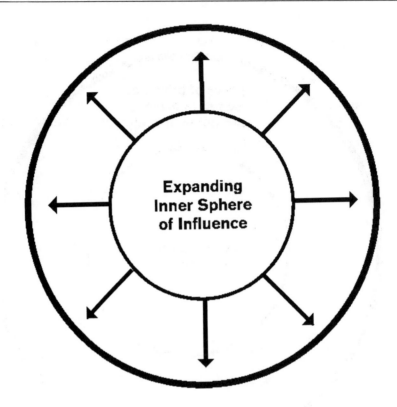

You expand the inner sphere by exploiting each of the seven promotional tenets covered in this book. If properly applied, each tenet expands your influence within your organization. Here's how it works. First, you need to identify your promotional strategies and fit them into a master plan. I'll show you how to do that in Chapters 1 and 2. In Chapters 3 and 4, you will learn how to sell yourself in any given situation, and maintain a high level of personal motivation at the same time. Motivation is the fuel you'll use to power yourself up the corporate ladder. You'll need to know how to communicate your ideas in crisp, concise terms along the way (Chapter 5). You'll also learn how to conduct exceptional meetings and presentations that will lock in the attention and respect of anyone in the audience. You need to aggressively network your way through your organization to get the attention of key decision-makers; I'll cover this in Chapter 6. Are you a great team player? You better be if you want to get promoted, so make sure you read

Chapter 7. Because you're bound to encounter some people problems along the way, I'll show you how to manage your way through conflicts and people obstacles in Chapter 8.

Although I recognize that anybody who buys this book certainty knows something about each of the seven tenets I cover, I want to make sure you know how to apply them to your maximum advantage. And I want you to understand how each of the tenets fits into your promotional strategy.

You'll also have an opportunity in the first chapter to take a self-test to identify your promotional strengths and weaknesses. I'll show you where to go in the book if you need help and how to access a whole library of "get ahead" ideas as well. I've even marked certain paragraphs with icons to make them stand out. They are:

? *Help* icons flag handy information that enables you to further understand the problems and solutions covered in a section. It may refer you to other chapters in the book, offer helpful tips, or point you toward outside reading material for complex problems.

● *Warning* icons caution you to pay extra attention to key issues presented in a section. Warnings tip you off to potential career pitfalls if certain critical situations are ignored or improperly handled.

Idea icons suggest alternate solutions or thoughts to problems covered in a section, depending on your unique situation. It's my way of providing alternative strategies for complex problems.

Because much of *1,001 Ways to Get Promoted* can be applied to a variety of settings, you'll constantly refer to it to find strategies that best fit your immediate needs. The guidance it offers will dramatically improve your success at achieving both your professional and personal goals. Good luck!

Chapter 1

Your Promotional Plan

Early in President Reagan's first term, his Commerce Secretary, Malcolm Baldridge, stated that executives are "fat, dumb, and happy." Baldridge's comment received lots of adverse press coverage, which prompted the *Harvard Business Review* to publish a study that concluded that top executives had an average IQ of 130 and were anything but dumb. Baldridge later clarified what he meant: "Many top executives lack vision and strategies to promote themselves and their organizations." When Baldridge made his initial comments in the early 1980s, the country was going through a period marked by corporate floundering, waste, poor quality control, and dismal productivity. Foreign competition was dominating the scene and in the early stages, many execs didn't have the foggiest notion of what to do about it.

As we entered the 1990s, all of that began to radically change. The mighty IBM corporation provides us with a classic example. The company, run by CEO John Akers, was the industry leader in mainframe computers. The fact that mainframes were obsolete and were rapidly being replaced by mid-range and powerful personal computers did not register with Akers or his executive staff. Akers' lack of a long-term promotional strategy for himself and IBM cost him his job. When Lou Gerstner took over as IBM's new CEO in 1991, he announced his personal strategy to promote IBM and put the company back on track. And, as radio legend Paul Harvey would say, "You know the rest of the story." Today, IBM is a highly successful strategy-driven company because Gerstner knew precisely where he wanted to go, how to sell his ideas and promote IBM's business.

In this chapter, I'll help you identify promotional strategies that will get you where you want to go. But first, you must answer the question: "Where do you want to go?" To help you answer, I've provided several examples to help you sort through your options. I'll show you the promotional tools you can use to get there and demonstrate how to use them. You'll also have an opportunity to take a candid self-assessment test to help you identify your promotional strengths and weaknesses. After you take the test, you can then focus on areas where you may need improvement.

Where Do You Want to Go?

Where do you want to go? What do you really want to do? How are you going to get there? These are three tough age-old questions we have all asked ourselves, and hopefully, have gotten better at coming up with realistic answers as we've gotten older. I assume you are reading this book because you want to move higher up in the corporate food chain by getting yourself promoted. Promoted to what? You need to be specific to know how to get there.

Thomas Edison offers a classic example of a man who knew exactly where he wanted to go, what he wanted to do, and how he was going to get there. While he was in the process of promoting himself to become an inventor, a young reporter asked him a question: "Mr. Edison, how does it feel to have failed 10,000 times in your present venture?" Edison replied, "Young man, I have not failed 10,000 times as you suggest. I have successfully found 10,000 ways that will not work." Edison estimated that he actually performed more than 14,000 experiments in the process of inventing the light bulb.

Like Edison, you need to determine as precisely as possible, where you want to go so that you won't lose focus on what will inevitably be a bumpy road to get there. Here's an example that illustrates what you should be looking for. Let's assume you're currently the manager of a sales organization and your goal is to become the senior vice president of sales. That's where you want to go. To get there, you need to get promoted to sales director, the position that reports directly to the senior vice president of sales. This would place you in a pivotal position to get promoted to vice president. That's how you are going to get there.

What about the "Is this really what you want to do" follow-up question? I encourage you conduct a "sanity check" on yourself to make sure this is truly the promotion that you want. Continuing with the previous example, project yourself into the position of senior vice president of sales. Consider all of the pros and cons of the job. Ask yourself hard questions, such as, "Are you willing to put up with the additional travel that goes along with this position?" When you're promoted into an executive job, you're expected to know everything it takes to perform at 100 percent capacity on Day One. Nobody is going to teach you what to do or show you how to make tough decisions. Are you prepared to take on the additional pressure that goes with this position?

If you have a confidant, someone whom you trust, now is the time to tap him or her for an objective opinion. He or she may reinforce your thoughts or introduce a different twist that perhaps you hadn't considered. Seek out the thoughts and advice of close family members and keep a log of everything you uncover relative to where you see yourself going. In the final analysis, you are the only one who can make the final decision. Is this where you want to go and what you really want to do?

? *Help:* Brian Tracy's book *The Great Little Book on Personal Achievement* (Career Press, 1997) is great reading for anybody who is interested in fulfilling their personal and career goals.

The 7 Promotional Tenets

In the Introduction, I established the seven promotional tenets you must master to mount a successful promotional campaign. In this section, you'll have an opportunity to take a self-assessment test to help determine what your current level of expertise is in each of the seven tenets. Before you take the test, let's briefly review the tenets with an emphasis on why they are important to the promotional process.

Tenet #1: Organizing. To get yourself promoted, you've got to have a solid strategy in place as well as a plan to implement it. If you're not well-organized, you'll substantially reduce your chances of getting promoted.

Tenet #2: Selling. Successful people are excellent salespeople. They know how to sell themselves and their ideas. You, too, must be able to sell yourself as you walk through the promotional process to get ahead.

Tenet #3: Motivating. The task of climbing up the corporate ladder is a tough challenge. You're going to slip along the way, and there will be plenty of roadblocks that you'll have to clear. You have to be capable of keeping yourself and others motivated on a perpetual basis if you expect to make it.

Tenet #4: Communicating. If you can't communicate effectively, in a manner where people can understand and appreciate what you're saying, your promotional ambitions will be severely handicapped. Your ability to conduct dynamic and productive meetings will reward you with favorable recognition.

Tenet #5: Networking. Your promotability will depend on who you know. You must establish a solid network of supporters and decision-makers on whom you can count.

Tenet #6: Teaming. The popularity of relying on teams to solve crucial business problems has returned to America's corporate scene. If you can demonstrate that you're not only a team player, but a damn good one, you'll make it to the top.

Tenet #7: Managing. Everybody in any organization must address human relations conflicts on a recurring basis. It's a fact of life. If you want to become an effective leader, you must know how to manage your way through people obstacles and business problems.

Although I have implied that each of the seven tenets stands on its own, it's a misconception. Each is interdependent on the other. For example, the fact that you may know how to communicate well is important, but it's even more important that you know how to use the right words when you attempt to sell your ideas. Organizing yourself is an important tenet that touches on all of the other six tenets.

(?) *Help:* Best-selling author Barbara Sher shows you how to define your dreams and attain them in her book *It's Only Too Late if You Don't Start Now* (Delacorte, 1999).

Taking the Test

It is my intent to supply all of the tools (tenets) you'll need to get ahead and to show you how to use them. I recognize that that's an ambitious undertaking, but if you stay with me until the last chapter, I'll help you make it happen. Let's take a moment and conduct a reality check. No human being can become a master at exercising to perfection every one of the seven promotional tenets. Because of the varied backgrounds of different individuals, levels of experience, chosen professions, and educational backgrounds, some people will be more proficient than others at exercising each of the tenets. For example, a successful sale manager will probably know how to sell himself or herself better than other professionals who are not involved in direct sales.

Therefore, I've created a Promotional Attributes Test that you can use to measure your proficiency in each of the seven tenets. Using the test results as a guide, you will then be able to determine which of the tenets to concentrate on and which ones you can spend less time with.

For each question on the test that follows, there are three answers from which to choose. Make sure you answer each question as best you can, even if some of the questions seem highly subjective, controversial, or don't apply to your current situation. Good luck!

Promotional Attributes Test

1. Do you smile when you greet your subordinates or associates?	1. Not usually 2. Sometimes 3. Almost always
2. Do you shake hands with a firm grip?	1. No 2. Sometimes 3. Yes
3. Are you unwilling to poke fun at yourself among your associates when you make a mistake?	1. No 2. Sometimes 3. Yes
4. Do people feel uncomfortable when they meet with you to discuss a problem?	1. Yes 2. Sometimes 3. No
5. Are you committed to making a team member out of anyone you work with?	1. No 2. Sometimes 3. Yes
6. When you talk to associates, do you finish their sentences for them?	1. Often 2. Sometimes 3. Seldom
7. Do you reject the notion that positive thinking is an attitude you can cultivate in yourself?	1. Yes 2. Sometimes 3. No
8. Do you find yourself engaged in hopeless causes?	1. Often 2. Sometimes 3. Seldom
9. Is it difficult for you to admit to your associates that you are ignorant about a subject?	1. Yes 2. Sometimes 3. No
10. Do you consider brainstorming with your associates a waste of time?	1. Yes 2. Sometimes 3. No
11. Do your associates think you are thin-skinned?	1. Yes 2. Sometimes 3. No
12. Do you have a confidant in your organization with whom you can share your most candid thoughts and emotions?	1. No 2. Sometimes 3. Yes

13. Are you eager to be the messenger who brings bad news to the boss?	1.Yes 2. Sometimes 3. No
14. Do your associates regularly seek you out for collaboration on projects or questions they might have?	1. No 2. Sometimes 3. Yes
15. Do you make little-known associates into supporters by taking them into your confidence?	1. No 2. Sometimes 3. Yes
16. Do you worry about trusting people too much?	1.Yes 2. Sometimes 3. No
17. Do your associates think you do not trust others?	1.Yes 2. Sometimes 3. No
18. Do your associates think you welcome their new ideas and initiatives?	1. No 2. Sometimes 3. Yes
19. Do you avoid making decisions without the approval of a higher authority?	1.Yes 2. Sometimes 3. No
20. Do you avoid making decisions that are controversial?	1. Yes 2. Sometimes 3. No
21. Are you willing to make tough, unpopular decision when you know they are right?	1. No 2. Sometimes 3. Yes
22. When you must oppose a group decision, are you willing to take the heat?	1. No 2. Sometimes 3. Yes
23. When you take the initiative, are you willing to move out of your comfort zone?	1. No 2. Sometimes 3. Yes
24. Does hindsight show you that your decisions have been right?	1. No 2. Sometimes 3. Yes
25. Do you spend your time looking good rather than being good?	1.Yes 2. Sometimes 3. No
26. Are you good at finding problems in your organization that need to be resolved?	1. No 2. Sometimes 3. Yes

27. Do your goals often turn out to be wishful thinking?	1.Yes 2. Sometimes 3. No
28. Do you maintain a healthy threshold for emotional pain when things aren't going your way?	1. No 2. Sometimes 3. Yes
29. Do you fail to learn and grow from your mistakes?	1.Yes 2. Sometimes 3. No
30. When adversity strikes, do you believe that things will eventually go your way?	1. No 2. Sometimes 3. Yes
31. Do you laugh when the joke is on you?	1. No 2. Sometimes 3. Yes
32. Do you like to needle your associates with critical hints rather than stating criticism directly?	1.Yes 2. Sometimes 3. No
33. Do you draw praise from your peers and management for your work?	1. No 2. Sometimes 3. Yes
34. Do you distinguish between wishes and desires when you plan your personal goals?	1. No 2. Sometimes 3. Yes
35. If given the chance, do you run from adversity?	1.Yes 2. Sometimes 3. No
36. Do you have difficulty picking yourself up after a business loss, such as losing out on a promotional opportunity?	1.Yes 2. Sometimes 3. No
37. Do you see yourself as a willing participant in a collaborative management process?	1. No 2. Sometimes 3. Yes
38. Do you think your job fails to make the right demands on you?	1.Yes 2. Sometimes 3. No
39. Do you make it clear to others in your company that you are available to help them on projects they undertake?	1. No 2. Sometimes 3. Yes
40. Do you maintain a daily schedule on a personal or hand-held computer?	1. No 2. Sometimes 3. Yes

41. Do you maintain a daily schedule in a daily planner, or other form of manual planner?	1. No 2. Sometimes 3. Yes
42. Do you have more than one goal that you are trying to achieve?	1. No 2. Sometimes 3. Yes
43. If you have goals, have you written them down and do you have completion dates established for each goal? (Answer no if you do not have any goals.)	1 . No 2. Sometimes 3. Yes
44. Have you ever been involved in direct sales either on a part-time or full-time basis for more than one year?	1. No 2. Part-time 3. Full-time
45. How would you rate sales as a profession?	1. Low 2. Medium 3. High
46. How would you rate your average level of motivation most of the time?	1. Low 2. Medium 3. High
47. Do you get upset if things aren't going your way?	1.Often 2. Sometimes 3. Seldom
48. Do you feel inspired when you arrive at work in the morning?	1. Seldom 2. Sometimes 3. Most of the time
49. Do you know a person whom you can call outside of your organization if you need help in solving any work-related problem?	1. No 2. Sometimes 3. Most of the time
50. How would you rate the overall merit of your work-related ideas over the past year?	1. Low 2. Medium 3. High
51. When you are confronted with a major work-related problem, are you one of the first to find a solution?	1. No 2. Sometimes 3. Most of the time
52. When you present ideas to your boss, how well are they usually received? (If you are not currently employed, answer questions 52, 53, 54, and 55 relative to the last job you had.)	1. Poor 2. Fair 3. Good
53. How would you rate the management capability of your boss?	1. Low 2. Medium 3. High
54. How would you rate the overall competency of the executive staff in your organization?	1. Low 2. Medium 3. High

55. Do you like your job?	1. No 2. Sometimes 3. Most of the time
56. When someone is talking to you, do you listen to what he or she has to say first, before you speak?	1. No 2. Sometimes 3. Most of the time
57. How difficult is it for you to call a peer and ask him or her for help?	1. Very difficult 2. Sometimes difficult 3. Not difficult
58. Do you like to attend meetings?	1. No 2. Sometimes 3. Most of the time
59. Do people understand what you are saying?	1. No 2. Sometimes 3. Most of the time
60. Do you believe that meetings are worthwhile?	1. No 2. Sometimes 3. Most of the time
61. If asked to make a presentation on the spur of the moment, how well would you perform?	1. Poor 2. Fair 3. Good
62. How important do you feel most business presentations are in your organization?	1. Not important 2. Somewhat important 3. Very important
63. Do you have an established network of business contacts that you actively maintain?	1. No 2. Sometimes 3. Yes
64. When you write a complex report, do recipients understand what you are saying in the report?	1. No 2. Sometimes 3. Most of the time
65. How often do you contact someone in your business network? (Answer "Seldom" if you do not have a business network.)	1. Seldom 2. Frequently 3. Very frequently
66. When you attend a company function, do you make it a point to talk to a least one member of upper management?	1. No 2. Sometimes 3. Most of the time
67. How would you rate your level of comfort when you attend a large company social function?	1. Low 2. Medium 3. High

68. How would you rate your level of comfort when you attend a small company social function?	1. Low 2. Medium 3. High
69. How comfortable are you if you're introduced to someone at work whom you have never met?	1. Not comfortable 2. Comfortable 3. Very comfortable
70. Is it difficult for you to maintain a conversation with people you do not know?	1. Yes 2. Sometimes 3. Not difficult
71. How would you rate the overall quality of your writing skills?	1. Low 2. Medium 3. High
72. How are you at delegating work?	1. Poor 2. Fair 3. Good
73. Do you like to delegate work to others?	1. No 2. Sometimes 3. Yes
74. How do you rate your ability to resolve conflicts with your subordinates or associates?	1. Low 2. Medium 3. High
75. How do you rate your ability to resolve conflicts with your boss or upper management?	1. Low 2. Medium 3. High
76. You have been asked to write an article for the company's newsletter. Will you accept the assignment?	1. No 2. Maybe 3. Yes
77. How do you rate your ability to delegate work to your peers?	1. Low 2. Medium 3. High
78. How would you rate your ability to negotiate a contract on behalf of your organization?	1. Low 2. Medium 3. High
79. How would you rate your ability to resolve a conflict with an irate customer?	1. Low 2. Medium 3. High
80. How do you rate your ability to negotiate an equitable settlement on a problem with one of your peers?	1. Low 2. Medium 3. High
81. Do your peers listen to what you have to say when you talk?	1. No 2. Sometimes 3. Most of the time

82. How important are teams in your organization?	1. Not important 2. Important 3. Very important
83. If you were assigned to a team working to solve a tough problem, how would you rate your level of participation?	1. Low 2. Medium 3. High
84. In your opinion, are work teams worthwhile?	1. No 2. Sometimes 3. Most of the time
85. Do you feel that you usually get credit from upper management for the work you perform?	1. No 2. Sometimes 3. Most of the time
86. Your boss wants you to make a presentation about diversity in the organization at the next staff meeting. How will you do?	1. Poor 2. Fair 3. Good

How Did You Score?

There were three possible answers for each question, and each answer was assigned a 1, 2, or 3 numeric value (that is, the number of your answer). To determine your level of promotional readiness, add together the numbers you checked for each question to arrive at your total test score. Make sure you answered all of the questions to the best of your ability. After you have added all of the numbers of your answers, compare your total score against the table below to see how well you performed. For example, if your total score was 210, then your score is "Good" relative to your overall ability to apply all seven tenets to get yourself promoted.

Total Promotional Tenets Test Score

Promotional Readiness Ratings	Score Range	Your Score
Superior (90% – 100%)	Above 232	
Good (80% – 89%)	206 – 231	
Average (70% – 79%)	181 – 205	
Fair (60% – 69%)	155 – 180	
Poor (Below 60%)	Below 155	

Your total score is a general indication of how proficient you are at applying all seven tenets to get ahead. If you were fortunate enough to have scored "Good" or "Superior," you are well on your way toward mounting an aggressive promotional campaign. If you scored somewhere below "Average," don't despair—that's why you bought this book. I'll help you identify the specific areas that you need to work on to become an expert at directing your own promotional campaign.

To determine your level of promotional readiness in each one of the seven tenets, total your score by adding together your answer numbers for the questions that are listed next to tenets in the tables that follow.

Organizing Skills Readiness
(Score questions 5, 8, 10, 12, 19, 24, 25, 26, 27, 29, 33, 34, 38, 39, 40, 41, 42, 43, 65, 72, 73, 78, 80, and 81)

Organizing Tenet Test Score		
Promotional Readiness Ratings	**Score Range**	**Your Score**
Superior (90% – 100%)	Above 65	
Good (80% – 89%)	58 – 64	
Average (70% – 79%)	50 – 57	
Fair (60% – 69%)	43 – 49	
Poor (Below 60%)	Below 43	

Selling Skills Readiness
(Score questions 2, 3, 4, 6, 7, 11, 13, 14, 19, 20, 21, 24, 25, 27, 28, 29, 30, 32, 35, 37, 38, 39, 44, 45, 48, 52, 56, 70, 71, 81, 82, and 83)

Selling Tenet Test Score		
Promotional Readiness Ratings	**Score Range**	**Your Score**
Superior (90% – 100%)	Above 86	
Good (80% – 89%)	77 – 85	
Average (70% – 79%)	67 – 76	
Fair (60% – 69%)	58 – 75	
Poor (Below 60%)	Below 58	

Motivating Skills Readiness
(Score questions 1, 3, 5, 7, 8, 13, 15, 16, 17, 18, 20, 21, 23,
25, 27, 28, 29, 30, 34, 36, 42, 43, 46, 48, 50, 51, 55, 61, and 85)

Motivating Tenet Test Score		
Promotional Readiness Ratings	**Score Range**	**Your Score**
Superior (90% – 100%)	Above 78	
Good (80% – 89%)	70 – 77	
Average (70% – 79%)	61 – 69	
Fair (60% – 69%)	52 – 60	
Poor (Below 60%)	Below 52	

Communicating Skills Readiness
(Score questions 2, 3, 6, 9, 12, 13, 14, 15, 16,
17, 18, 20, 21, 22, 25, 26, 28, 30, 31, 32, 35, 39,
44, 47, 52, 56, 58, 59, 60, 61, 62, 70, 82, and 84)

Communicating Tenet Test Score		
Promotional Readiness Ratings	**Score Range**	**Your Score**
Superior (90% – 100%)	Above 92	
Good (80% – 89%)	82 – 91	
Average (70% – 79%)	71 – 81	
Fair (60% – 69%)	61 – 70	
Poor (Below 60%)	Below 61	

Networking Skills Readiness
(Score questions 1, 2, 4, 5, 6, 9, 10, 12, 14, 15,
16, 17, 18, 25, 26, 31, 32, 33, 36, 39, 44, 45, 46, 49,
56, 57, 58, 59, 63, 65, 66, 67, 68, 69, 70, 76, and 81)

Networking Tenet Test Score		
Promotional Readiness Ratings	**Score Range**	**Your Score**
Superior (90% – 100%)	Above 100	
Good (80% – 89%)	89 – 99	
Average (70% – 79%)	77 – 88	
Fair (60% – 69%)	66 – 76	
Poor (Below 60%)	Below 66	

Teaming Skills Readiness

(Score questions 1, 3, 5, 6, 9, 10, 13, 14, 18, 20, 21, 26, 28, 29, 30, 32, 35, 37, 39, 49, 52, 56, 57, 59, 60, 70, 71, 82, 85, and 86)

Teaming Tenet Test Score		
Promotional Readiness Ratings	**Score Range**	**Your Score**
Superior (90% – 100%)	Above 81	
Good (80% – 89%)	72 – 80	
Average (70% – 79%)	63 – 71	
Fair (60% – 69%)	54 – 62	
Poor (Below 60%)	Below 54	

Managing Skills Readiness

(Score questions 1, 4, 6, 7, 19, 20, 21, 23, 24, 25, 26, 27, 28, 29, 33, 35, 38, 41, 50, 51, 53, 54, 56, 74, 75, 76, 77, and 79)

Managing Tenet Test Score		
Promotional Readiness Ratings	**Score Range**	**Your Score**
Superior (90% – 100%)	Above 76	
Good (80% – 89%)	67 – 75	
Average (70% – 79%)	57 – 66	
Fair (60% – 69%)	50 – 56	
Poor (Below 60%)	Below 50	

For each tenet, compare your test score against the scores in each table to determine areas where you may need improvement. I recognize that the promotional readiness test is highly subjective, but it will give you a realistic indication of the areas you need to work on to improve your chances of getting promoted. In the remainder of this chapter, I offer several ideas on how you can best leverage your strengths and minimize your weaknesses. At the end of the chapter, I'll show you how to pull it all together into a promotional plan to help get you started.

Leveraging Your Strengths

If you've ever watched Chis Everet play tennis, you would notice that this great tennis player could have improved her game by coming to the net more often. Everet knew that she couldn't be good at everything, and she didn't try to be. Knowing what her strengths and weaknesses were, she defied conventional wisdom by working on her strong points first, and only working on her weak points when she had time. If you look at top performers in any field, including business, they aren't good at everything they do. They're usually great at a few things, which gets them to the top of the corporate ladder.

The test helped you identify your strengths—the areas that you can exploit to get yourself promoted—and your weaknesses. Take a moment and list on a piece of paper the promotional tenets where your strengths lie and then prioritize your tenet scores from high to low. When you have completed your prioritized list, answer the following questions, which will help you develop a strategic plan for your promotion:

1. **What tenets are important in your current job?** Rank the seven tenets from high to low with respect to relative importance to your current job. Compare this ranking with the ranking of your test scores. Identify those tenets that are important to your current job where you scored below "Good" on the test. These are the ones you will want to work on first. They will not only enhance your current job capabilities, but your future job opportunities as well.

2. **What do you think were the major qualities, characteristics, and strengths that enabled you to do well over the past year?** For example, if you formed a team to help resolve a major problem and the team accomplished the task to the delight of upper management, then note your success in the teaming area and any of

the other six tenet areas that you can think of. Now, list four or five activities that you like to do in your spare time and be as specific as you can. For example, if you like to play golf, what specifically do you like about the game? Is it the social aspect of the game or the precision that's required to drive a ball off the tee?

3. **What best qualities do the activities that you listed in Question 2 bring out in you?** For example, if teaming brings out your sense of accomplishment, then make a note of that fact. If social qualities are what golfing brings out in you, make a note of it. Often seemingly unrelated work and pleasure qualities can provide you with information that you may overlook when you develop your tenet strengths.

4. **What tenet strengths do you have that you're not using in your job?** For example, if you're a good team player, are there ways that you could become more actively involved in teaming within your organization? What are some of the opportunities you could potentially realize if more of your tenet strengths were applied to your current job? If you were to rewrite your job description to better utilize your strong points, what would it look like? Write a paragraph that redefines your job so that it leverages your strong points.

Now, sit back for a moment and reflect on what you have written relative to the questions. Is there anything that would prevent you from modifying the way you're currently approaching your job to incorporate part or all of your revised job description? For example, if you're a great communicator and you have determined that you do not have the opportunity to make many presentations in your current job, what can you do to change the situation? Perhaps you could volunteer to present the status of a key project at the next staff meeting.

Here's another example. Let's assume that you scored high on networking, a tenet that was partially reinforced by the social qualities you enjoy from golfing. However, in your current job, you don't have an opportunity to establish a network that would be conducive to your promotional ambitions because you're chained to your desk. How can you leverage your networking strengths to help you get ahead? Suppose two of the people you need to get to know better who can influence your promotion are organizing the company Christmas party. Volunteer to help them out. This will give you an opportunity to get to know them better.

Develop a list of everything you can do to apply your tenet strengths in areas that will improve your odds of getting promoted. If you go back to the Chris Everet story, remember what she did to become the number-one tennis player in the world: She concentrated on perfecting and utilizing her strengths first, before she worked on improving her weaknesses.

It's now time to write a job description for the position that is the target of your promotional objectives. Before you begin, get a copy of the current job description from human resources so you can refer to it for basic job requirements. If none exists, create one based on what you know about the job. Does the job utilize your tenet strengths to the max? Are there tenet strengths that you should be using, but for whatever reason, aren't? Will your current job, as well as the one you'd like to get promoted to place demands on you in any of the tenet areas where you are not strong? What can you do to improve your strengths in these tenet areas?

Before we move on to the next section, document five distinct aspects of your tenet strengths that you'll use to get yourself promoted. To help you get started, complete the exercise that follows.

1. List each tenet prioritized from most important to least important relative to succeeding in your current job. Highlight any tenet that's on your list where you scored below a "Good" rating.

2. List each tenet prioritized from most important to least important relative to getting the position or job that you want. Highlight any tenet that's on your list where you scored below a "Good" rating.

3. Make a note of any tenet that's listed in the top five in numbers one *and* two above where you scored below a "Good" rating. These are the main tenets that you should work to improve as they are important to the success of your current and future jobs.

The Promotional Attribute Test helped you identify tenets where you may not be as strong as you would like to be. Take a moment and determine if your lack of expertise in any of these tenets is causing you problems on your current job. If your answer is yes, then place a check mark by each appropriate tenet and briefly identify why you are having problems with each.

Repeat this same exercise, but this time place a check mark next to each tenet that you believe will be important when you're promoted to the job you want. Refer to the job description you wrote in the previous section. If any of the tenets on your "weak" list have two check marks by them, move them to the top of your work list. The lack of expertise in any tenet that is holding you back in both your current and future jobs cannot be ignored. If, for example, you need help in communications, get it! Read everything I covered in this book on the subject and check out the outside readings I recommend.

Creating a Game Plan

Before I show you how to put it all together into a promotional game plan, let's first define what I mean by a game plan. The most basic of all game plans is designed to leverage the strengths and minimize the weaknesses of the players. You are the sole player in the game of getting yourself promoted, and like all players, you have strengths and weaknesses that you bring to the game. As we discussed earlier, you need to maximize your strengths and minimize your weaknesses to get promoted.

Find a place where you can be alone and uninterrupted to read the next few pages. Clear your mind of everything except what you will read and what I encourage you to do. Don't worry about your schedule, your business, your family, or your friends while you work on this section because I want you to focus on what you need to do to create a promotional plan that will assure your success.

Start your promotional game plan off with the end results in mind by picturing yourself in the position that you're striving to obtain. Assume that you have just been promoted and you're walking into your first staff meeting. Be extremely positive. What are your subordinates thinking about you? What character traits would you like them to see in you that's making a difference in their jobs and lives? Why do they want to work for you and how can you keep them constantly motivated? Are you making major contributions to the company by meeting or exceeding all of your goals? Before you read the next paragraph, take a few minutes to jot down your thoughts on each of these questions.

The visualization experience that you just went through allowed you to touch some of the deep fundamental values you'll bring to the table as you climb up the corporate ladder. Now, it is time to assess if you have possession of the right tools to make the climb. To help you complete the planning part of your promotional campaign, let's return to the salesman who wanted to become senior vice president and review the game plan he created:

1. Our salesman knows where he wants to go. He's currently a sale manager for XYZ Corporation and he wants to mount a campaign that will put his career on the fast track and get promoted to senior vice president of sales.

2. His score was 185 from the Promotional Attributes Test, which I have shown in the chart that follows.

Total Promotional Tenets Test Score		
Promotional Readiness Ratings	**Score Range**	**Sales Manager Test Scores and Rating**
Superior (90% – 100%)	Above 232	
Good (80% – 89%)	206 – 231	
Average (70% – 79%)	181 – 205	185
Fair (60% – 69%)	155 – 180	
Poor (Below 60%)	Below 155	

3. Our salesman has summarized his tenet strengths in order of proficiency (high to low).

Tenet Attribute Ranking (High to Low)	**Sales Manager Test Scores and Rating**
Selling	Superior
Organizing	Good
Motivating	Good
Communicating	Average
Networking	Fair
Managing	Fair
Teaming	Poor

4. Our salesman has reviewed his current job and believes that the following promotional tenets are critical to his success in order from high to low. He's also recorded his respective test score for each tenet:

Promotional Tenets Critical to Current Job (High to Low)	
Tenet Description	**Sales Manager Test Scores and Rating**
Selling	Excellent
Managing	Fair
Teaming	Poor
Motivating	Good

5. Our salesman reviewed the job he wants (VP of sales) and believes that the following promotional tenets are critical to his success in the new position, which he ranked in order from high to low according to his test scores. You have also recorded your respective test score for each tenet:

Promotional Tenets Critical to Future Job (High to Low)	
Tenet Description	**Sales Manager Test Scores and Rating**
Managing*	Fair
Teaming*	Poor
Networking	Fair
Selling*	Excellent
Organizing	Good

* Indicates tenets that are important to both current and future job positions.

Our sales manager identified the critical tenets that he needs to take into consideration to form a game plan to get himself promoted to vice president of sales. He identified tenets that were critical to his current job and to his future job opportunities and ranked them in order from high to low. The tenets at the top of his list represent the tenets that he must rely on to get himself promoted. If you have been following up to this point, you should have a comparable list that relates to your situation. It's now time to implement your game plan.

Your current plan should call for a way to leverage your strong points that are not currently being exploited. For example, if you scored high on your ability to communicate, a function that you're not utilizing to your fullest capability in your current job, figure out a way to leverage this strength to your advantage. How? Let's assume that you're an excellent communicator and know how to negotiate deals with the best of them. Suppose you discovered that the procurement department is swamped with more pending contracts than they have time to negotiate. You believe that the vice president of procurement would be a valuable ally to have in your network because she is someone who could help get you promoted. You subsequently meet with her to offer your assistance to help negotiate key contracts. In this scenario, you potentially kill two birds with one stone: You leverage one of your untapped communication skills (negotiating) and network yourself into the good standing of the VP of procurement.

Your development strategy may call for a plan to improve upon a key tenet weaknesses you believe you have. Let's assume that you hate selling anything, including yourself—a conviction that was reinforced by your dismal selling skills score on the attributes test, as well as at the last staff meeting when you tried to sell the group on one of your great ideas. Unfortunately, the position you're seeking demands lots of carefully worded sales-oriented presentations that you'll be required to make to the CEO and the board of directors on a regular basis. One of your development strategies might be to take a selling skills course at a local university or community college.

Start Hitting Home Runs

IDG Publishing has added another book to their *Dummies* series titled *Baseball For Dummies*, which can be summarized in one sentence for those of you who either don't like baseball or don't want to buy this excellent book. You'll learn that strikeouts are bad, any hit is good even if it's an out, and home runs are great. If Babe Ruth were alive today, he'd tell you that's basically all you need to know when you go to a baseball game.

Did you know that Babe Ruth began his baseball career as a pitcher and set a record of 29 scoreless innings in 1918, a record that would remain unbroken for 43 years? He also set another record of having more strikeouts in his career than any other baseball player in history. And yet, when you think of Babe Ruth, you don't think about his awesome pitching record, you think of the number of home runs he hit. While most players were just trying to get on base, Babe Ruth hit more home runs in the number of games he played than anyone else in the history of the game because home runs were the only thing that counted as far as Babe Ruth was concerned.

Sometimes we all get caught up in that same pattern where we just hope to get on base and not suffer the embarrassment of a strikeout. Whether it's in our personal relationships or our career pursuits, we don't want to rock the boat. Even Little League coaches will tell the kid who's up at the plate with a three-ball, two-strike count, "A walk is as good as a hit!" When I was in Little League, a walk never felt as good as a hit, even if the hit was caught for an out.

In 1920, Babe Ruth hit more home runs for the New York Yankees than the entire number of home runs hit by any of the other teams combined. Shortly after the end of the season, Yankee Stadium was built and became know as "the house that Ruth built." There are three basic reasons why people might be willing to settle for walks and base hits when they could be hitting home runs:

1. They don't believe they're capable of hitting home runs.
2. They don't know how to hit a home run.
3. They don't like to take risks so they'll settle for a hit or walk instead of a home run.

Let's return to our Babe Ruth story to find out what he did to overcome the three most common excuses people use to not hit home runs in their personal and professional lives. Babe loved statistics. When he discovered that according to the statisticians, only 3 percent of the population used a goal-setting program to achieve their objectives, and the 3 percent that did set goals earned, on average, twice as much as those who didn't set goals, he instantly decided to join the 3-percent club. Babe set a goal to get himself "promoted" to the best baseball player in his time, and he did it!

Idea: Joe E. Lewis, 14-year heavyweight boxing champion, once said, "You only live once, but if you work it right, once is enough."

Implementing Your Plan

Implementing is one of the most powerful action verbs in the English language and it's also the most difficult thing for most people to accomplish. Creating an action plan is relatively easy to accomplish, but successfully implementing the plan that you have created is a whole different matter. At the very heart of the circle of influence that I discussed in the Introduction is your ability to make and keep commitments to yourself, which also forms the essence of your promotion. Through your human endowments of self-awareness, you become conscious of your areas of strengths and weaknesses, areas of improvement, and areas where your talents can be immediately applied to your current promotional plan. I've shown you how to sort through your strengths and weaknesses, and offered you several thoughts on how to set priorities to create a winning promotional game plan that's right for you.

When you implement your promotional plan, you will begin to establish an inner integrity that will give you an awareness of self-control, courage, and the strength to accept more of the responsibility for your promotion. The power to make and keep commitments to yourself is the essence of the planning process and a prerequisite to your promotion. You've got to be well-organized if you expect to implement a sound promotional plan. I'll introduce you to organizing, the first of the seven tenets, in the next chapter.

Idea: Frame yourself. Decide what you want to be known for. What matters to you most and where do you want to have the greatest impact? It will give people a frame of reference of who you are and what you're good at doing. Are you a good people person? Do you like to come up with creative ideas to solve impossible problems? Maybe you like to develop systems that get things done. Listen to what your instincts tell you and focus some of your energy on areas that are important to you and your promotional objectives.

● *Warning:* Everybody experiences failures during their career. Show me a person who says they've never failed, and it will be someone who has never taken a risk. They're a failure for not having failed—and they are probably lying! As we read, Edison went through 14,000 different filaments before he found one what worked. He didn't let any of his thousands of failures dissuade him from his task. You must have the same fortitude as you drive to promote yourself. Have fun in the process and consider your encounters with failure all part of the adventure.

⑦ *Help:* Do you remember the movie *City Slickers* when Jack Palance told Billy Crystal, "There is only one thing that can cause your success in life"? When Billy asked, "What's that" Jack held up his finger as a gesture for him to seek the answer on his own. By the end of the movie, you hopefully discovered the answer. For the benefit of those of you who didn't see the movie, the answer was that every human being under extreme circumstances has the innate power to apply multiple skills that they didn't believe they had.

Chapter 2

Organizing Yourself

The Wizard of Oz was truly a great and inspiring movie. All Dorothy had to do was follow the yellow brick road and she would get to Oz, where all her prayers would be answered. The movie reminds me of the job market in the 1980s when everybody got promoted on a regular basis. You didn't have to do anything to get promoted other than to just be there. God forbid if you wanted to implement a change that would disrupt the way things had always been done. It was one of the quickest ways to kill your promotional opportunities.

Now that the 1990s are behind us, I'm sure you've noticed that the yellow brick road has been torn up and replaced with a new speedway. Those poor souls who still thought they were on the yellow brick road got run over as corporations moved at lightning speed to "right-size" themselves, disrupting careers and lives in the process. You either survived the cuts, learned how to work harder, or were put out to pasture with the other sacred cows and bulls. We've all been there, done that, and we sure don't want to go back to Oz.

Even though you may still have scar tissue on your backside, you can't help but ask yourself, "What do I need to get myself promoted in a tougher competitive environment and to continue my climb up the corporate ladder?" In this chapter, I'll help you walk through the critical organizational issues that you'll need to address to get ahead of the pack and get yourself promoted. If you're not organized, and I mean organized to the point where you can run as efficiently as a fine-tuned Indy 500 race car, your chances of achieving your promotional objective will be substantially reduced.

Why Organization Is Critical to Your Success

We all know we need to be organized, but what exactly does "being organized" mean? We tend to bind the definition in qualitative terms like: "I'm organized because I always know what I am doing and where I am going." When you ask the person who makes this statement to show you his or her master plan, you'll quickly realize that in most cases, the organizational plan is made out of fluff. Nothing in the so called "plan" has been written down, goals are not clearly defined, and you'll be hard pressed to find anything that resembles a schedule.

If you're not well-organized to the point where your plan is documented in writing and supplemented with some kind of dynamic daily, weekly, or monthly tracking system, your chances of meeting your promotional objectives will be reduced by 80 percent or more. It'll just end up being words piled upon words, backed up with lots of lame excuses. An organizational plan that's worth its salt is made up of actions and goals that can be measured to determine it you're on track.

You must be willing to subject yourself to benchmarks that will let you know if you're on the right track and headed in the right direction. The task of getting yourself promoted is a complex process that has to be worked every day of the week. With rare exception, nobody has the mental capacity to keep in their heads everything they must do plus register the myriad of daily feedback they must process that will help them get there.

(?) *Help:* You'll discover the laws that govern success, money, happiness, and organization when you read Brian Tracy's book, *The Great Little Book on Universal Laws of Success* (Career Press, 1997).

Start With Goals

Goals are what generates the fuel that drives your self-directed promotional plan. Unfortunately, it is easier for most people to just rattle off a set of goals because words are cheap, and as the saying goes, the road to hell is paved with broken promises. For every goal that actually gets completed, there are a million that never get started. To avoid this pitfall, think about the following statement: "The future drives the activities of the present!" Bill Gates saw the future in a little computer program called DOS. IBM didn't. Gates methodically established goals that would promote him to where he wanted to go, and you can rest assured that he is following this same path today.

Unfortunately, goals often get confused with objectives. In our salesman example, his ambition of getting promoted to vice president was an objective and not a goal. Goals are the steps you must take to reach your objective. If you don't have precise, clearly defined goals, you will never make it to your objective. You'll be like a ship without a rudder drifting in the sea rather than heading toward a specific destination you've marked on a map.

John Fabre, the great French naturalist, conducted an unusual experiment with processionary caterpillars. These caterpillars would blindly follow the one in front of them and, hence, were called processionary caterpillars. Fabre carefully arranged them in a circle around the rim of a flowerpot and placed pine needles, their food, in the center of the pot. The caterpillars started following each other around the circular flowerpot day after day until they dropped dead of starvation. With an abundance of food less than six inches away, they starved to death because they confused activity with accomplishment.

Many people make the same mistake when they set goals, and as a result, reap only a small fraction of what life has to offer. Despite the fact that untold promotional activities lie within their reach, they remain stagnant in their positions because they blindly follow the crowd in a circle to nowhere. That's because the only goals they have are the ones they invent in their heads on a moment's notice when someone asks them what their goals are. The pursuit of meaningful goals is essential to the promotional process, because the successful completion of goals provides the rewards needed to achieve your ultimate promotional objective.

In Chapter 1, I identified a number of promotional tenets that our hypothetical sales manager felt he needed to master to achieve his objective of becoming vice president of sales. How does he incorporate goal-setting to augment his strategic objective? We know from the summary data that he was weak at communicating (making presentations), which was hindering his progress in his current job and handicapped his promotional prospects. It might make sense for him to establish a goal within some defined time frame, like three months, of becoming proficient at preparing and making presentations. The "how he's going to do it" part of his plan should be broken down into specific tasks and events that may include activities such as attending a seminar on the subject or joining a Toastmasters group.

How will he know if he achieves his goal of becoming proficient at making presentations? Perhaps he plans to make a formal presentation in front of his peers three months from the day he creates the goal. He plans to ask them to rate the quality of his presentation by completing a questionnaire he's designed for this purpose. Whatever *your* goals may be, it's important that you address what you want to accomplish. Your goals then provide you with a sequential plan to get you to where you want to go.

Adopt Your Organization's Mission

Organizational goals are shared conceptions of the intention, purpose, or objectives of the organization. Such goals may be stated in bylaws, charters, policy statements, or even printed on the back of employee business cards. They are often presented in very broad terms and may be called mission statements or purpose statements. They are sometimes stated in more definitive terms, like objectives. Organization goals answer the questions as to why the organization exists and what it is trying to do. To illustrate how organizational goals work and how you can interact with them to improve your image within the organization, let's see how they're used at Western Industries.

Western Industries is a long-established manufacturing firm with a mission statement that's printed on the back of every employee's business card. It reads: "Our mission is to become the market leader in the production and distribution of heavy extraction equipment." To achieve its mission, the company has created a number of goals designed to increase its market share of dump truck sales by 6 percent. (Once you become familiar with your organization's mission, you're in a much better position to establish your work priorities so that they are in alignment with the goals of your organization.)

For example, suppose you have developed a unique promotional idea that, if implemented, would help sell more of Western's dump trucks. You introduce your idea at an executive staff meeting with the opening statement, "Ladies and gentlemen, in keeping within the framework of supporting our mission to increase dump truck sales, let me share one of my ideas with you." Look what you have accomplished by playing on two important promotional tenets, organizing and communicating: First, you have shown that you are well-organized because you are directing your efforts at achieving an important company goal. Second, your opening statement was a "presentation attention grabber" because you effectively told the executives that you have an idea that will help them achieve their mission.

Idea: Conduct three five-minute goal reviews every day. Spend five minutes every morning reviewing your routine goals and what you intend to do during the day to help meet those goals. Routine goals are a continuation of what you are already doing or are expected to do. Spend another five minutes every afternoon reviewing goals that will help you resolve problems. What can you do today to eliminate immediate problems? Then spend five minutes every evening reviewing personal goals and what you have done today to help meet tomorrow's goals. These review exercises don't take a lot of time and they will help you focus on your goals.

Warning: If you don't have an active set of goals that you are religiously pursuing on a regular basis, you will cripple your chances of ever getting promoted. Goals are made up of all the subtasks that you must complete to move up in any organization.

Be the Best You Can Be

How do you feel about the idea that people have lots of potential they don't use? It's easy to see how it applies to others, but not you, right? For most of us, it's an uncomfortable experience to look for our own areas of untapped potential. And yet, we know intuitively that we are not performing up to our true potential. Have you ever said to yourself, "I know how to do that so why did I blow it?" If it helps, you're not the only person who ever had that thought.

William James, American psychologist, said, "People only use about 10 percent of their potential, which is probably high." Even if you're not average and are using more than 10 percent of your potential, there is still a gap between your true potential and your actual performance. Although that thought may be difficult for you to confront, it's a giant first organizational step you must be prepared to take. It will increase your chances of getting promoted and assure your success once you get there.

Have you ever gotten the feeling that you were about to embark on one of the most important trips of your life? When this feeling hit you, did you suddenly understand where you were going and how you were going to get there? The clarity of what you must achieve was overwhelming and you were confident of what you must do. If you have had this experience, you've reached what psychiatrists call a breakthrough. It enables the winner within you to break out and achieve your most important goals.

Can you get excited about the idea of being the best you can be? I'm not talking about being better or more successful than someone else, because that's a relative measurement that doesn't mean anything. You know who you are and how good you are today. The really exciting challenge for any of us is to take charge of ourselves and become the best we can be.

Warning: Have you acquired any new skills lately? Are you more entrepreneurial today than you were at this time last year? Have you mastered decision-making, and just how much value have you added to yourself over the past 90 days? If you haven't acquired at least one new skill over the past six months, then you're going to have a difficult time getting yourself promoted unless you can hide the facts from those who are responsible for your promotion. The challenge to get yourself promoted is to build your skill set, which is not just another nice idea. It's critical to your career because your profitability depends on such achievement. If you avoid growing, avoid the responsibility of stretching yourself, and avoid being truthful about your strengths and weaknesses, you'll find yourself on the outside looking in. Make no mistake, this is a global drift. You must become an achiever, committed to work teams, taking risks, balancing your skill set, and obtaining results if you want to get promoted.

Develop Your Full Potential

Before we discuss techniques you can use to develop your full potential, let's first define a few terms. What exactly is potential? Potential is the accumulation of all your inborn talent and acquired knowledge, and the motivation you have to drive the productive use of your mind, body, and soul. Although I believe that everybody is born motivated, people often act as though they are not. In many cases, there's something going on in their lives that's limiting their inborn potential to excel, to be motivated.

If everybody really wanted to use their potential to the fullest, why doesn't it happen? Why does the salesperson sit and stare at the telephone for 30 minutes before finally calling a prospect? Why do you rush to complete your tax return at the very last minute when you've had several months to work on it? It's all because the human system is primarily an emotional system. Positive emotions tend to enhance the flow of whatever potential a person has. Negative emotion, like the emotion caused by the negative task of completing one's tax return, blocks that flow. If you identify areas in your life that are really working, they are probably in areas where you have developed very positive feelings about what you are doing. You're applying positive emotions rather than negative emotions to get the job done.

Let's take a look at the other side of the coin. What was the negative emotion that kept our salesman from picking up the telephone? Most likely, it was fear. Fear of failure, fear of rejection, or perhaps a combination of both. Why do you sometimes wait until the last minute to complete an assignment? Perhaps you were mad because you shouldn't have been given the assignment in the first place, or it's your way of striking out at a boss you can't stand.

All of these examples reflect normal human emotion. Unfortunately, if they are allowed to build up in your system, they can take control of your behavior, prevent you from performing at your best, and ultimately stop you from getting promoted. Negative emotions block the flow of potential. Have you ever driven a car with the emergency brake on? Recall how you felt when you suddenly realized what you had done and reached down to release the brake. All of a sudden, your car started to run normal again as you quietly chewed yourself out for not releasing the brake before you started to drive.

Here's the parallel. We all drive through life with our emotional emergency brakes on to solve problems—we clinch our fists and repeatedly tell ourselves we'll try harder to do things better. We've all tried that system and most of the time it doesn't work. Unfortunately, trying harder can backlash and raise your frustration level to record heights. A better approach is to become familiar with your emotional braking system and learn how to release the brakes to allow your potential to flow. Let's look at six techniques you can use to develop your full potential:

1. Grow like a weed. When people stop learning, they start to die. People who excel are excited about learning and growing to become the best they can be. Do you like to learn new stuff? Do you have a personal library of self-improvement books in your home that you read on a regular basis? Do you listen to educational and motivational tapes when you drive to work in the morning? When you attend a training program or seminar, do you head for the front row so that you can hear everything that's said? Decide right now to learn everything you can.

2. Develop self-esteem. Self-esteem is your feeling of value and significance. It's different from self-confidence where you know you can do something. Self-esteem is the degree to which you're in the habit of acknowledging that you are a good person, and you excel at what you do. One way to enhance your self-esteem is by recalling times when you have felt a sense of pride and accomplishment and say, "If I did it then, I can sure as heck do it now." Boost your self-esteem by forbidding yourself from ever wallowing in past failures and thus reinforcing negative events. Instead, treat learning from your mistakes as a positive experience and get on with the next challenge in your life.

3. Find a support group. You can build self-esteem by joining formal and informal support groups. A formal group may be a trade association. Informal groups may include your family and friends. In a group setting, you build self-esteem by giving some of yours to another person, and in return, you'll receive some of theirs. Try it by finding simple, direct ways of helping the people you know feel better about themselves. When people feel good about themselves because of you, they will do anything for you.

4. Learn to love pressure. One of the interesting patterns we see today in top executives is their positive attitude about pressure. They love it! Learn to absorb any demands that come your way. Deadlines, tough problems, and the need to adapt to changes can all be viewed as stimulating opportunities. People who have developed the habit of perceiving pressure as a positive force are the ones who get promoted.

5. Become an optimist. Another key to your excellence is the ability to find joy in everything you do. People who have an optimistic outlook on life are catapulted out of bed in the morning because of their high energy levels. They know how to make it through the day with a good sense of humor and are fun to be around. As a result, people actively seek them out for advice and to take on challenging assignments. They're also healthier than pessimists because positive emotions contribute to physical health.

6. Become accountable. People who are comfortable with the fact that they are accountable for the consequences of their behavior and decisions excel in higher-level positions. They're constantly reinforcing what they know works and correcting what doesn't work. Conversely, people who are low on the accountability scale seldom get promoted. When things go well for them, they won't know why, but they'll grab all of the credit they can get. They'll always look for someone to blame if things go bad.

Over the next week, focus your attention each day on one of these six techniques to develop your full potential. Start your day off with the determination that you are going to expand yourself in at least one specific area. As your day progresses, look for opportunities to practice using positive attitude attributes on people to see the positive effects it has on them. Check your progress at the end of the week. You should see important, positive changes that are moving you toward realizing your full potential and that promotion you want.

Idea: Winners know how to exploit their full potential because they are always part of the answer. A loser is always part of the problem. A winner has a goal. A loser has an excuse. A winner says, "Let me do it for you." A loser says, "That's not my job." Winners always see the green near every sand trap. Losers see only sand. Only winners get promoted!

Think Positively

In the process of getting yourself promoted, you'll face pressure and anxiety-provoking situations. You'll deal with tight deadlines, confront strong competition, and have meetings with back-stabbing peers, and you'll have to digest more information than your brain wants to process. Fast-trackers understand that the best way to stay on top of the heap is to always keep things in their proper perspective. There'll be times when you have to pat yourself on the back for a job well done because nobody else will. There will also be times when you'll have to kick yourself in the butt for making dumb mistakes.

No one bats a thousand. Unfortunately, many of us have an unconscious tendency to dwell on our loses and take our wins for granted. If you focus on the negative and exclude the positive, you will develop a false assessment of how things are going for you. When that happens, you risk getting into a vicious cycle that'll reinforce your feelings of inadequacy. If you continue to dwell on your mistakes, you'll start doubting your ability to handle any job, including the one you're driving for.

Periodically perform a follow-up analysis on yourself. Balance your losses with your wins to get an accurate overall view of how well or poorly you're doing. Chances are you are doing better than you thought you were. However, if you truly believe you've lost ground, don't hide the facts. Carefully evaluate what you did wrong and what you can do to correct the situation. If you determine that it's all "water under the bridge" and there is nothing you can do to correct or change the situation, get on with the rest of your promotional plan. Winners are willing to acknowledge their mistakes, which doesn't bother them because they're always learning from them. Treat the situation as a learning exercise and get on with the pursuit of your goals.

(?) *Help:* Norman Vincent Peale shows you all kinds of ways to apply positive thinking in everything you do in his classic book *The Power of Positive Thinking.*

Keep Your Priorities Straight

Polish the stone but don't try to reshape it. Everyone has been on the receiving end of the conventional wisdom that is constantly warning us to become more efficient, get organized, or risk becoming obsolete. However, if you try to plug all of the holes in your promotional plan, you may become extremely frustrated. It can distract you from perfecting your other strengths, from polishing the stone.

Here's a classic example of what I'm talking about. Dan is my partner, and his desk always looks like Hurricane Elva just hit it, which drives me crazy because my desk is the picture of perfection. Everything has its place to the point where you can blindfold me and I can still find my stapler because it's been in the same spot on my desk for the past 10 years. Following conventional wisdom, I convinced Dan that it was time to clean up his act. To help him get organized and make better use of his time, I hired a consultant to follow him around for a day and make some recommendations. At the end of the day, the consultant gave Dan a weekly planner, showed him how to use it, how to set priorities, and how to organize his desk. The consultant was trying to reshape the stone.

After following the regime for a month, Dan was just a little bit more organized, complained of headaches daily, and his billable business had declined by 25 percent. He also became impossible to get along with. In desperation, the two of us got together at the local bar and several beers later, both of us simultaneously realized that he was never going to be well-organized. From that point on, Dan's desk returned to its traditional sloppy state, his daily planner started collecting dust in one of the desk drawers, and his billable business was back to where it should be. We both learned that the most important part of organization is keeping your priorities straight. The quantitative side of organizing does not have to be pretty as long as you methodically work your priorities. Polish the stone instead of trying to reshape it!

⊘ *Help:* Managing time is an age-old concern that affects those who have too much to do and not enough time to do it right. Everyone could use more hours in a day to accomplish their goals. Brian Tracy's *The Great Little Book on Mastering Your Time* (Career Press, 1997), gives practical, stimulating guidance on how manage your time like an expert.

Don't Lose Your Peripheral Vision

Have you ever been in a restaurant and tried to get your server's attention, but couldn't? After he brought you a steak, you noticed that he forgot the steak sauce. And you wanted that glass of wine you ordered with your meal, not when you've finished. Maybe you were in a hurry and just wanted the check. What made this situation especially annoying was that your server was scurrying all around you, but for some reason you couldn't catch his eye. He didn't make use of his peripheral vision. He didn't want your eyes to meet with his, which would force him to acknowledge your request for more service.

Many people are just as incompetent as this server, except that their poor performance is not limited to the self-imposed blinders they choose to wear. They'll also refuse to speak up on an issue that demands their support. Have you ever had a teacher or college professor who answered questions nobody was asking? They're bent on providing information nobody wants rather than providing information that's needed. They also lack peripheral vision.

Don't allow this same thing to happen to you as you move up the corporate ladder. You may feel that you are so busy doing whatever your boss tells you to do that, like the server, you don't have time to turn on your peripheral vision. Take the time in a quiet moment to think about what you're doing and seek out imaginative ways to support what your organization wants done. If you do this right, you'll stand head and shoulders above the rest of the crowd. Remember, they can't promote you if they can't see you.

Idea: Ask five people you trust and whose opinions you respect to tell you what they think are your greatest professional weaknesses. Then ask them to identify your greatest natural talents, the things you do well when you are in a social setting. Do your professional weaknesses relate to your natural talents? For example, if articulate communications is one of your professional weaknesses but you have a natural talent talking to people in a social setting, find a way to integrate your natural talent into your work to compensate for your weakness. It may help you expand on capabilities that you didn't know you had.

Hang onto Your Integrity

Integrity is the cement that must be in place to assure your promotion. According to Webster's, integrity is composed of completeness, soundness, and unity. A skyscraper needs integrity to stand tall, and so do you. Integrity means not compromising yourself and taking the high road whenever you can. What's the high road? It's sticking with the right decision even though you know it may not be the most popular decision.

Why is integrity important to your promotion? If it is perceived by those who are responsible for promoting you that you don't have any integrity, you will not get promoted. If you are promoted and they discover after the fact that you don't have any integrity, you may subsequently be fired. When you step into a greater leadership role, you will be making decisions that involve greater risks than what you're making today. Your integrity will become a critical factor in evaluating the criteria for making the right decision.

If you haven't been promoted to where you think you should be, then take a hard look at your integrity. Maybe your integrity is not as strong as you think it is. If you're one of those people that always likes to keep your mouth shut and duck making your opinion known on tough issues, then the problem may be that nobody who counts knows what your integrity level is or—even worse—they may even doubt your integrity. Your integrity is at risk when you're not telling yourself or someone else the truth. If you break your word, you lose a chunk of your integrity. Every flaw in your integrity will rob you of a chance to get promoted. Here's how to conduct your own integrity test:

1. Identify at least five recent situations where your integrity has been less than ideal.
2. Carefully think through what your rationale was that caused you to compromise your integrity for each situation identified in #1.
3. What was the outcome of each situation that you identified in #1?
4. How would you have approached each situation identified in #1 if your had practiced integrity?
5. Would you have been better off in the short-run if you had not compromised your integrity?
6. Would you have been better off in the long-run if you had not compromised your integrity?

I sincerely hope that when you got down to number six on the integrity check list, you concluded that you would have been better off had you used integrity in everything you did relative to the situations you identified in number one. Although you may have been better off by not practicing integrity in the short run, you would have suffered in the long run. If you walk away from this exercise concluding that integrity is not important, good luck!

Rely on Your Intuition

Brain scientists tell us that we only use about half the capacity of our brains. Our respective lack of use of intuition is a major contributor to our half-wit capacity. And yet, top CEOs and executives will tell you that their best decisions are based on intuition. Although intuition is regarded as better than a hunch, it is difficult to link it to logic. Intuition is based on some level of knowledge that cannot be denied. Although everybody has intuition, there are only a few who will actively acknowledge their intuition and act on it. Here are three things you can do to develop your use of intuition:

1. Be creative. Take at least 15 minutes a day to be in complete creative silence. Find a location where you are free from interruptions and distractions. You don't need to do anything during this time except to be in touch with yourself, something we often forget to do. Your creative time can run the gamut, from just staring out a window to meditating. The whole idea of the exercise is to get you to start feeling clearer about your own ideas with a sense of ease and confidence. You'll start getting answers to questions that you have been pondering for some time.

2. Frame your questions. The way you frame the questions you ask yourself to qualify your intuition is very important. If your questions are too subjective, you will not be able to validate what your intuition is telling you. For example, "Should we hire this person?" may be too vague. If you ask, "What are the strengths and weakness of this person?", you're more likely to get specific information that you can use to make an informed decision. Avoid posing open-ended questions like, "Will I get promoted?" Yes, you will get promoted sometime in your lifetime. Ask yourself specific questions in order to use your intuition well.

3. Know the difference between intuition and fear. You need to learn how to differentiate between intuition and fear. Anything that's loud, jarring, frightening, or upsetting is more likely a feeling of fear than intuition. If your intuition needs to send you a warning, it will do so in a quiet, controlled way. For example, instead of stepping blindly into a street, something inside you cautions you to look first. As a large truck whisks by, you know intuitively that something inside told you to look first. Intuition is always gentle, which distinguishes it from fear. Conversely, fear compels us to make irrational decisions that are not blessed with any intuition.

Job pressures and the mistrust of your own capabilities all contribute to dampening your use of intuition. If you don't know how to rely on and trust your intuition to make decisions, you are going to have a difficult time moving up the corporate ladder.

(?) *Help: The Great Little Book on the Gift of Self-Confidence* by Brian Tracy (Career Press, 1997) helps you shed those insecurities that prevent achievement, success, and happiness.

Find a Vision

Nobody can become a real leader without vision. It's what you see for yourself that fuels your drive to promote yourself. You can't have direction within your organization if your people don't share your vision. A vision is a compelling image of an achievable future event. It may be grand in scope, but it is definitely achievable. It has to be bigger than you if you want others to help you achieve your vision, which means it has to be for the greater good of your organization.

For example, the vision at Insight Enterprises is to become the world's best company in the direct marketing of computer-related products. Insight's vision is printed on the back of every employee's business card. Everything this top-notch sales-oriented company does directly or indirectly supports their vision. It's the reason why they exist and why they get better and better at direct marketing every day.

What will your vision be when you get promoted? Becoming a great leader starts with you and your personal vision. Your vision can't be forced, because if it is, you won't follow it. If it doesn't come to you easily, let it go for the time being and focus on some other part of your promotional campaign. Find out how other people you know have created visions that have served them and their organizations well. Become infinitely familiar with the concept and the techniques you can use to make sure people will buy into your vision. They'll be compelled to follow your vision if they can relate to it and believe it's good for everybody.

Create a Long-Term Plan

Every company that's worth its salt has a five-year plan that gives it direction and keeps it on track to where it wants to go. You also need a personal five-year plan to give yourself direction. Start by contemplating what you will be doing five years from now and work back from there. How much money will you be making and what kind of office will you have? Where will you be living and who will you be working for? What kind of business will you be in and what will you be doing? What's your title and who will you report to? These are just a few of the questions you should ask yourself. Develop your own set of answers that identify realistically where you think you'll be five years from now.

Once you have your five-year plan written down, check to see if your short-term plan will help you get there. If it doesn't, then perhaps you're going off in the wrong direction, so you may need to modify your short-term plan accordingly. Following are a couple of pointers that will help you create a good long-term plan:

- ✓ *Think big.* Think big, but not so big that your chances of achieving your long-term goals are going to be next to impossible. Stretch your ambition as long as it's achievable.
- ✓ *Create your own dreams.* Dreams are what ambition is built on. So what if the position you really want doesn't

exist? If it fulfills a viable function, sell your dream to the CEO and you're on your way. It happens every day.

✓ *Map it out.* Make sure everything in your short- and long-term promotional plans fit together. Everything you do in your short-term plan should support at least one or more components in your long-term plan. If they don't, get rid of unnecessary activities and tasks so you're not wasting your time.

✓ *Increase your sphere of influence.* Incrementally begin to increase your sphere of strategic contacts. Every contact that you add to your sphere of influence must be able to directly or indirectly support your promotional efforts. If they don't meet that criteria, then they don't belong in your sphere of influence.

✓ *Challenge every component and task* that's in your promotional plan at least once a month. Ask yourself the question, "Will everything that's in my plan help me get to where I want to go?" If your answer is no, then modify your plans. If you never modify your plans, then something is wrong. Your plan is either too simple or it isn't challenging enough.

Protect Your Reputation

I often tell people who attend my seminars that business is one giant corporate game that you play to win. That advice, however, does not give you a license to win at all costs. Any player who will double-deal and cheat to win has no place in the game. Although it is possible to get promoted by playing this way, you will lose over the long-term. It's just a question of time when your reputation catches up to you, and when it does, nobody will want to work for you or worse yet, have you work for them. The powers-that-be who are responsible for your promotion will ultimately become aware of their error and dismiss you.

When you play by the rules, you must never forget that you will inevitably run into someone who lacks integrity and doesn't play by any rules. Be alert! A snake can take a healthy chunk out of your backside before you even know you've been bitten. These people can cost you a promotion and ruin your reputation. They can do it by spreading lies and unfounded rumors that are specifically designed to undercut your reputation. Once you loose your reputation, you're no longer promotable and you may even encounter problems keeping your current job.

Here's an example of how it can happen. When I wrote my book *The Corporate Game*, I hired Mr. Promise (not his real name) to transcribe hours of audiotapes that formed the basis of the book's text. The timely completion of the transcriptions was critical to meeting my publisher's deadline. Mr. Promise seemed to have his act together. His rates were competitive, his work samples were great, and he promised to complete the assignment in two weeks.

At first, he delivered as promised. However, within a few days, the work had deteriorated to where there were numerous typos and missing paragraphs in the copy. It was also clear that the job would not be completed as promised. Every time I approached this guy, he'd tell me that the job was 90-percent done, and when I returned the next day to pick up the completed work, it was still 90- percent done. In utter frustration, I paid Mr. Promise for his sloppy work, fired him, and found another transcription service.

A year later, I landed a government contract that would require massive transcription work to be performed. In keeping with government regulation, I placed a display ad in the local newspaper inviting transcription contractors to submit competitive bids. Mr. Promise called me, apologized for all that had happened on the previous job, and assured me that he now had his act together. When he asked me if I would consider his bid for the new work, I politely told him no thank you. It's relatively easy for one to destroy his or her reputation. It's extremely difficult to rebuild a lost reputation.

Learn to Love Mistakes

To err is human. No matter how much you anticipate the problems, do your homework. And be prepared, you'll still make mistakes. If you're taking risks such as heading up a challenging project or finding a solution to a tough problem, you'll make mistakes. Nobody learns to walk without falling. Nobody learns how not to make decisions without making mistakes.

The vice president of sales at Compaq Computers once told me that when he interviews prospective salespeople, he asks them about the accounts they've lost. "When somebody tells me they've never lost an account, I conclude that they are either lying or they never made a sale." Mistakes can result from inaction as much as from action, where the real mistake is procrastination. Examples include not buying that stock when you should have or failing to stand up to that idiot when everybody was watching. Waiting because you're not willing to take the risk won't get you promoted. When you wonder why someone else got promoted instead of you, it was probably because they were willing to take risks while you stood on the sidelines.

You can also learn more from your mistakes than you can from your successes. Once you accept this fact of life, you'll be more willing to step up to the plate and take calculated risks. Tennis pros do this all the time. They'll try a new shot, and hit the ball into the net. They'll review the fundamentals of the shot in their mind to determine what went wrong, make the necessary adjustments, and try the same shot again and again until it's perfected. Contrast this with players who are satisfied with figuring out how to just get the ball over the net and you're looking at the average players of the club. If you aren't making mistakes, you aren't growing and learning. Or, as one CEO put it, "If you're not making mistakes, then you're not making any decisions, and you're not worth promoting."

Other executives are echoing that same message because they recognize that mistakes are a natural and necessary part of the learning process. Rather than adopting the conventional attitude of fearing mistakes, many of them are encouraging and in some cases, demanding decisions out of their people that could and do result in mistakes. In a changing, unpredictable world, the irony is that not making enough mistakes risks your promotion and clearly leaves you at a disadvantage. Following are several examples of people who were willing to take risks, made mistakes in the process, and still got promoted.

IBM's founder, Tom Watson Sr., encouraged his vice presidents to take the initiative and develop new products. One of his young vice presidents took the initiate to develop a new product, which turned out to be a $10-million colossal flop. Watson summoned him to his office to discuss the loss and when the young man arrived, he handed Watson his letter of resignation. Watson was outraged and said, "What do you mean you want to quit? We just spent $10 million on one hell of an education! I can't wait to see what you're going to do next." Learning from his father, Tom Watson Jr. subsequently went on to steer IBM into becoming a multibillion-dollar international corporation that was beyond his father's wildest dreams.

In the late-1960s, Chrysler Corporation had turned into a dinosaur. Every car it produced was obsolete and consumers actively referred to them as "running bucket of bolts that might not get you across town." The number-three auto maker in the country was on the verge of going bankrupt. Out of desperation, the board of directors found an ex-Ford executive named Lee Iococca who agreed to become Chrysler's CEO. Lee immediately had Toyota Corollas installed in glass cases in front of the entrances into Chrysler's plants with a sign that read in big bold letters for the workers to see, "If we can't build a car at least as good as this, kiss your job goodbye." Today, Chrysler is one of the premier car manufacturers in the world.

Scandinavian Airlines (SAS) president Jan Carlzon told his employees, "I want you to make mistakes. I know you are all so good that for every wrong mistake you make, you'll make 20 or

30 good decisions that will carry you and our company into the future."

Tom Peters, author of management books such as *Thriving in Chaos,* put the right spin on the word "mistake" when he said, "The essence of innovation is the pursuit of failure, and one's ability to try different things and not be concerned about making mistakes. The assumption that all great leaders shared is that we all need to experiment, innovate, and be daring in our thinking. You can't be innovative and not make mistakes."

Idea: Those who cannot remember their failures from the past are condemned to repeat them.

Think Big

When you set goals, something inside you should say, "Let's get going. What are we waiting for?" Setting goals is like laying the bricks that will form the foundation of your promotion and pave your way to a prosperous future. Because it's your future, why not think big? Everybody else who has gotten anywhere religiously set big goals and met most of them to get to where they wanted to go. Why should you be any different? Here's how to set yourself up with meaningful goals:

Goals must be big. In order for a goal to be effective, it needs to be big enough to create excitement within you enough to make you want to accomplish the goal. There's no excitement in just keeping up with someone. The excitement comes from doing your best or better than you think you can to accomplish something you really want. That's the whole purpose of a goal. It's an established fact in the sports world that athletes perform better against tough competition. This is the reason why many upsets occur, like in football when a "nothing" team beats a highly ranked team. The same is true in business. If your goals are challenging and tough, they will bring out the best in you.

Mix short-range goals with long-range goals. Short-range goals are less than six months, and conversely long-range goals are more than six months. You need to pursue short-range goals to keep your enthusiasm and motivation in high gear. Nothing is more invigorating than being able to tell yourself, "Well, I finally did it. I met a tough short-range goal and it feels good." To balance things out, compile your short-range goals with long range goals. One of the advantages of setting long-range goals is that they can neutralize frustrations you may encounter while pursuing short-range goals. For example, your long-range goal may be to become the vice president of your organization. Suppose you set a short-term goal to pass the CPA exam to help you get there, and you fail the first exam. Yes, you are frustrated but, in view of your long-range goal, it's only a temporary setback. You have time to figure out what you did wrong and take the exam again.

Work your goals daily. Goals are made up of work tasks. When you successfully complete all of the tasks in a goal, you've met your goal. If you don't have a daily plan to work your goals, you qualify as a dreamer. Dreamers set goals but have no plans or intentions of working them. They are the ones who tell you, "Someday I'm going to be financially independent. I've got a great plan but I haven't had time to work it yet." The late Charlie Cullen, turn-of-the-century-entrepreneur-turned-millionaire, expressed the need to consistently work on goals when he said, "The opportunity for success does not come cascading down like a torrential rainfall, but rather it comes slowly, one drop at a time. Work your goals every day and they will become a reality."

Goals must be specific. If they are made up in generalities, you'll never know if you ever complete one. In the previous example, I used the goal of becoming financially independent, which was not a specific goal. To qualify as a specific goal, dollars should have been added to the objective so that the person who set the goal would know when he or she actually achieved the goal of becoming financially independent.

Goals must be realistic. If you set goals that are unrealistic, and as a result, you consistently miss them, you could seriously impact your ability to achieve any goal. It could even affect the degree that you're willing to set new goals because of your high failure rate. Although I encourage you to set challenging goals, make sure they're reachable. If your goal is to apply for a job where there are 500 applicants, make sure you keep the goal in its right perspective. Even if you are without a doubt, the most qualified candidate, the odds of meeting this goal are against you because of the sheer number of candidates.

Goals must be yours. Any goal you set must be yours. If you have set a goal only because you are trying to please someone else, then it's not a goal. It qualifies as an assignment. If someone else is directing your goal, it's highly unlikely you will be 100 percent behind it, which will hamper your effort.

Everybody's goals should be directed at helping them do the best they can each day while they prepare for a better tomorrow. Your daily accomplishments are what you must do to achieve the goals you've set in place to assure your future.

(?) *Help: Seize the Day,* by Danny Cox and John Hoover (Career Press, 1994), is written for anyone who is interested in making high performance a regular part of his or her daily life.

Never Give Up

George Foreman once said, "You only fail when you give up." When you know in your own mind that you have given something your best effort and it's not working out, don't quit. Simply start another project. Years ago, a friend of mine invited me to join him in a new startup business to sell a gadget that we were convinced millions of people needed. It didn't take me long to discover that nobody wanted it, so I got out of the business in the nick of time. My friend unfortunately pursued the sale of our gadget until the bitter end and lost several thousand dollars in the process. When it was all over, he told me, "You know, Dave, I hate to lose money but the thing that really concerns me is the fear that this experience will make me overtly cautious. I'll be afraid to consider other viable business opportunities. If that happens, then my loss will be multiplied many times over." How true!

One man didn't let that happen. He was initially involved in an oil venture that ran out of money and oil. He left the oil business and started a clothing store, which didn't do any better than his oil venture. As a result, he went broke, but he wasn't discouraged. Later on in his life, he got involved in politics. Historians are already saying nice things about Harry S. Truman, the two-time failure who kept getting back up and became a United States president.

As you continue your journey to the top, you must remember that each rung in the ladder is placed there for the purpose of holding your foot just long enough to allow you time to step up to the next higher rung. It wasn't put there as a footrest. Joe E. Lewis said, "Although we all get tired and discouraged when things are tough, you fight one more round if you want to be the champion. A second wind isn't good enough. You'd better have a third, fourth, or as many winds as it takes to win."

There's an enormous amount of surplus reserve in each of us. But it's worthless unless you know it's there and use it. Persistence and effort are vitally important to your promotional campaign.

 ⑦ *Help: Promoting Yourself in the Workplace* (Careertrack Inc., 1997) by Jeffrey Magee talks about never giving up and shows you how to move professionally up the corporate ladder. You'll learn how to showcase your talents and abilities to get yourself promoted.

Become a Seeker

Seekers are constantly on the alert, scanning the horizon, and probing to find exactly what they're looking for, which often is a promotion. They usually find whatever it is they want, and even if they don't succeed, their quest enlarges their perspective. In a very real sense, you too are a seeker because you're trying to find a way to get yourself promoted, and like all good seekers, share a common attribute. You are eager to learn from seekers. If you're working for a boss who believes in you and supports your drive to get promoted, then you've already got a good mentor. Once you accept a mentor into your fold, you will have to be prepared to accept their criticism and the demands they'll place on you to get you up to speed for your promotion. If you don't have a mentor, take the initiative to seek one out.

In your search, be alert to your weaknesses that need nurturing. Identify three or four people who have the credentials to bring you along in these areas. Then, find a way to get to know them and ignore any hesitancy you might have about seeking them out. Choose the ones who are most appropriate to meeting your needs and convince them that it's worth their while to invest time in you.

Idea: The one person who's always happy to teach you a lesson is a tough competitor. Seek out whatever your competitors can teach you every chance you get.

Get Passionate

Passion isn't restricted to love. If it's applied right in any one area of your life, it will affect every other area. When you are passionate about anything, it gives you more vitality, energy, and purpose that will transfer into your life's goals and objectives. Jerry Madden, one of my best friends, was a runner for years until he injured his knee. He had it operated on and the doctor told him he'd have to find another sport that was easier on his knees. He subsequently took up biking.

Jerry told me, "After about a year of riding a bike, I realized that I was only 20 minutes off the qualifying time for Colorado's Continental Divide bike race. It was like someone lit a fire inside me. I started getting up at four in the morning and biking 25 miles before I went to work. I'd do the same thing when I got home at night. My excitement and passion for biking carried over to my job. I went from being in the middle of the sales force to the top sales-person and was promoted to district sales manager. I qualified for the Continental Divide bike race and did well for my age. My passionate life is incredible."

When you have passion in your heart, it lifts your entire life. Days go by faster and your work becomes more interesting. You'll have more stamina, more resiliency, and more buoyancy in everything you do. Passion takes you from merely being competent to being outstanding. Fueling the passion and fire in your heart is an important step toward getting yourself promoted. Here are four thoughts that will help you get passionate:

1. A recent nationwide cross-industry study found that the one distinguishing factor between top and good performers was their amount of enthusiasm.

2. TV sports analyst John Madden said, "The difference between the guys who make the Pro-Bowl and those who don't is their passion for the game."

3. The prestigious *Endicott Report* confirmed that there are three critical qualities to job success: enthusiasm, motivation, and passion.

4. Holiday Inn founder Kemmons Wilson defined passion as an emotion that's infused with spirit. He said, "If you don't have passion and enthusiasm, you don't have anything."

Maybe you're excited about hiking, baseball, mountain biking, or doing charity work. Maybe your family makes everything worthwhile. The important thing is that you develop your passion and use it to build a fire in your heart. When that happens, nothing is insurmountable. You'll find that nothing is too hard, no peak is too high to climb, no dream is impossible to realize, and you'll enjoy the climb up the corporate ladder.

Idea: I believe after observing thousands of people that their inability to get organized is responsible for a majority of their failures to get themselves promoted. It's why otherwise bright people turn out to be mediocre performers and achieve only a small degree of the success they could achieve if they were organized. A disorganized desk, car, or way of life leads to confusion, a sloppy image, a poor attitude, and most of all, reflects to upper management that you're not promotable. List on a 3 x 5 card all of the things you need to do to get yourself organized, from straightening your personal things to improving your appearance. Pick an item off the card each week and do it. When you've organized everything you've got listed on the card, make up another card, where you'll list further ways to organize yourself.

Take Risks Not Chances

In today's business world, taking risks is not an option; it's mandatory if you want to get promoted. Nobody in their right mind is promoting non-risk takers. Just to survive, much less succeed, you must learn how to get out in front of the tide and make risky decisions. If you wait too long, someone else will do it for you, and you'll be stuck in the mud with the rest of the turtles. Your biggest risk is not to take risks.

One of the greatest risk takers of all time was Chrysler's Lee Iacocca, who said, "Most people are looking for security and a nice, safe, prosperous future. And there is certainty nothing wrong with that. It's the American dream. Yet their biggest fear is screwing up, their fear of failure, of not achieving the American dream. The fear of failure brings about the fear of taking risks. You're never going to get what you want out of life without taking some risks."

However, taking risks is not the same as taking chances, which was pointed out by sports psychologist Dr. Bruce Ogilvie who completed a research report several years ago that showed important distinctions between risks and chances. Ogilvie studied several risky occupations that included race car drivers and aerobatics pilots. He discovered that risk takers in dangerous professions spend an extraordinary amount of time planning and preparing for their activities. During an interview, he said, "These professionals analyze every factor that can go wrong to reduce risk and to eliminate chance. Such assiduous planning increases one's confidence, commitment, and helps them conquer what otherwise would be debilitating fears."

The key to successful risk taking is to understand that the actions you're taking should be the natural next step. One of the mistakes we often make when confronting a risk situation, whether it be learning a new skill or starting a new project, is our tendency to focus on the end result. Skiers who are unsure of themselves often do this. They'll go to the edge of a difficult slope, look all the way down to the bottom, and from where they are on the hill, determine that the slope is too steep for them to try. The ones that decide to make it change their focus by analyzing what they need to do to master the first step, like getting through the first mogul on the hill. Once they get there, they concentrate on the next mogul, and over the course of the run, they end up at the bottom of what others thought was an impossible mountain.

When you start something new, always figure out what you need to do to accomplish the task in logical steps. After you complete the first step, it becomes easier to take on the next natural step because of your increased confidence. As you progress, you'll keep moving in the right direction. Over time and given enough steps, you, too, will make it to the bottom of the mountain. Toyota uses the same "little step" thinking in their innovation program. While other companies strive for dramatic breakthroughs when they introduce new models, Toyota keeps doing lots of little things to better their cars every model year. They call it "rapid inching up." Over time, the inches add up and have allowed them to outdistance their competition.

(?) *Help: Simple Steps to Impossible Dreams* (Simon & Schuster, 1998) by Steven Scott is an excellent book that offers hundreds of ideas about what you can do to realize your dreams without taking any chances.

Find Criticism Before It Finds You

Webster's defines criticism as the act of evaluating or analyzing works of art or literature. If you consider yourself a work of art, then maybe you fall under the domain of Webster's literary definition. Mike Snell, my literary agent, told me when I first started my writing career over a decade ago that if I can't stand criticism, and in particular *his* criticism, I wouldn't last long in the writing world. At the time, I didn't know exactly what he was talking about, but over time, I have come to appreciate the true value of criticism. Simply put, without the benefit of criticism, my writing would not have improved over the years. I subsequently believe that nobody can improve at whatever they do if they are not fed a healthy dose of criticism on a recurring basis.

The use of criticism in the sports world offers a classic example. John Elway is one of the greatest quarterbacks of all time, and yet he has his own private quarterback coach. Why does John need a coach that costs several hundred thousand dollars a year? If you think his coach is standing around watching John practice all day long and telling him how great he is, you are mistaken. John's coach earns his money by criticizing him. You can almost see how the system works when he says, "John, here's the play, here's what you did wrong, and here's what you need to do to perfect the play. Try it again." If the best recognize a perpetual need for criticism, then so should you.

Idea: You don't need persistence to go downhill, but you can't go uphill without it.

Fight to Win

Pit bulls are truly amazing animals. My daughter and I were riding our mountain bikes into the red rocks of Sedona, Arizona when we came upon a couple who were hiking down the trail with two pit bulls. My mind instantly turned to the negative press pit bulls have received over the past several years. They've been branded as vicious attack dogs that will even attack human babies. We decided to get off our bikes and let the pit bulls pass to avoid a confrontation. The couple stopped to talk to us and before we knew it, we were talking about their pit bulls.

They told us that pit bulls are unusually friendly and mild-mannered dogs unless they are threatened or attacked. They went on to tell us that pit bulls were originally bred in the 1800s in England to fight with other dogs in pits, hence their name. They seldom lost a fight to another breed because they're extremely persistent. They would lock their jaws onto a vulnerable part of the other dog's body and just hang on until the fight was over. Have you ever heard somebody refer to another person as a pit bull? "He's a real pit bull. You can count on him staying with the job until it gets done." If you're persistent like the pit bull, you'll win most of the time. Let's review the steps you need to take to win most of the time.

Create a vision. Persistence begins when you create a vision. Share your vision with other people. Get them excited about what you're trying to accomplish and actively solicit their help. Form a team where everybody is unified and motivated by the same vision.

Demand criticism. With rare exception, no one likes criticism, but they should. Think about it. If, from this point on, you're never subjected to criticism, what would happen? You'd never get better at doing anything you're doing today. When you hire the golf pro to give you a half-hour lesson for $50, what are you doing? You're paying this person a lot of money to criticize the way you play golf so that you can get better.

Expect obstacles. If you don't expect to run into some obstacles and roadblocks while you're pursuing a goal, then it probably isn't much of a goal. Treat an obstacle as a challenge that will broaden your mind as you overcome the obstacle to get to where you want to go.

Be persistent. One of the greatest enemies of winners is his or her own impatience. Sprinters know that they have to go all out when they're running a 100-yard dash. Conversely, long distant runners know that they have to pace themselves to successfully complete a marathon. Unfortunately, worthwhile goals are never only a hundred yards away. They are usually at least a mile away, so pace yourself so that you can finish the race. Watch for burnout and mistakes that can occur if you don't control you pace. Learn to control your pace and you'll win every time.

Idea: Good employees do something without being told. They are the winners and the ones who get promoted.

Love What You're Doing

Bill Gates has an estimated net worth that exceeds $50 billion. If he and his wife spent $100 million a year, it would take them 500 years just to spend the principle. The interest alone would last him several hundred more years. So why show up at Microsoft and continue working every day? Why do other insanely rich people like Ted Turner, Oprah Winfrey, and Steven Spielberg continue to run on the corporate treadmill, day in and day out? The answer to the question is the reason why they got themselves promoted in the first place. They love what they're doing, and even when they hit the financial pinnacles of their careers, they refused to take their foot off the accelerator because they're having fun.

Truly liking whatever you do is what keeps everything in your personal and professional life moving forward. It's what drives your motivation, gets you out of bed in the morning, gels solid relationships, and moves you up rather than down the corporate ladder. I'm not talking about moments of passion, but continuous adrenaline that flows through your veins like blood. Do you like what you are doing? Better yet, do you love what you are doing? If you answered no, how in the world do you intend to fool anybody in your organization so that you can get yourself promoted? If you're that good, then maybe you should consider becoming an actor.

Unfortunately, there are a lot of people who don't like what they are doing. I once had a young man, Jerry, who worked for me and hated his job. Fortunately for the both of us, over a relatively short period of time, Jerry finally found something he loved doing. When I hired Jerry, I knew intuitively he was a winner. He had just graduated from college and was one of the brightest kids I'd ever known, but he didn't know what he wanted to do. Initially, I didn't care because he could write computer programs faster than anyone else in my company.

I bounced Jerry from one department to another in an attempt to help him find something he really liked doing, but nothing seemed to excite him. In desperation, I took him with me to a board meeting so that he could see how the real world operated. Jerry had an opportunity to see every step of the executive decision, making process, from quantifying problems and working out solutions with the other divisions, to developing strategic business plan objectives. Boy, was this kid jazzed.

On the way back to the office, I asked Jerry if he knew what he wanted to do yet. He told me he wanted to become an executive, a CEO of a service-based company like Computech. I didn't have this book to give him at the time, but I helped him develop a promotional plan that instantly became a passionate part of his life. Our parent company, Seattle First National Bank, promoted him to CEO of one of their subsidiaries before Jerry hit 30. He was the youngest CEO in the 79-year history of the bank.

Lots of people have been standing around all of their lives just waiting to find something they would like to do. When you ask them how they're doing, they are the ones that always mumble, "Okay I guess." There are several inherent risks that are associated with waiting around to figure out what you'd like to do. You're wasting your valuable time, crippling your motivation, and short-circuiting your promotional opportunities. If you ever find yourself in this position, watch what good job hunters do.

Hunters know they can greatly improve their odds of success by actively searching for something they'd like to do. The hunt itself becomes a passion to them. They'll latch onto something they like or love doing and are the first to tell you, "Hey, I love my job. It could become a real passion for me." They'll continue to work on developing what they love doing until they hunt down something they like even better.

Bringing passion into your promotional pursuit is critical if you want to hit the big time. Throughout all of recorded history, passion has driven the world's greatest leaders to the heights of human accomplishments in every imaginable field and endeavor. All winners have it and rely on it to get to where they want to go. So can you.

That's why I always turn to the sports page in the newspaper first, because it records what the winners have accomplished. The front page records nothing but mans' failures.

? **Help:** *Achiever's Profile* (AMACOM, 1997) is an excellent book written by Alan Cox that poses 100 achiever-oriented questions and answers to sharpen your promotional instincts.

Chapter 3

Selling Yourself

According to *Fortune* magazine, more than 50 percent of today's CEOs had a C average in college and more than 75 percent of U.S. presidents graduated in the lower half of their class. If numbers don't appear to be the barometers of success, then what makes a successful CEO? Highly successful CEOs are often the best salesmen or women in their organizations, which is how most of them got promoted to the position. Although your promotional objectives may not include becoming a CEO, you had better be darn good at selling yourself if you expect to have a reasonable chance of getting to where you want to go, regardless of how good you think you are. If you can't sell yourself or you can't learn how to sell yourself, you'll have a difficult time making it, because there is literally nobody else who can do it for you. The one interview question they'll always ask you is, "Tell me why you're the best person for this job?" You had better know how to answer with all the pizzazz of an excellent salesperson. I'll help you develop several excellent answers to this and other related questions in this chapter.

Idea: A three-word job description of a good CEO is BSP, or the Best Salesperson in the Place.

Sell Yourself With Pizzazz

A good promoter is always selling their ideas, a service, a product, or themselves. Business is a selling game every day of the year, 24 hours a day. All you have to do to test your selling powers is ask yourself at the end of the day, "Did I sell any of my ideas today?" If the answer is no, then ask yourself, "Did I try to sell anything?" If you come up with another no, you've got a problem—big time. Quite simply, you can't promote yourself if you aren't trying to sell yourself and your ideas every day. You can stand on a street corner with a box of new Rolex watches that you're selling for a dollar each, but if you don't at least say to somebody, "Do you want to buy a watch?" you'll never sell one.

Every sale you make is a point in your favor. And don't be afraid to bring some pizzazz into your sales pitch. Several years ago, I developed a way to increase the throughput of digital computer boards by a whopping 25 percent at one of IBM's manufacturing facilities. When I demonstrated my idea to several of IBM's directors, they were favorably impressed with the process and its cost-savings potential.

A week later, I found myself standing in front of IBM's executive review board that was responsible for reviewing and approving all major changes to a manufacturing process. When I completed what I thought was an excellent sales presentation, one of the execs asked me how much the new process would save? When I told her it would save $100 a minute, she instantly snapped back with the question I had anticipated, "Prove it!" I walked over to her, removed a $100 bill from my pocket, tore it in half, and gave her half of the bill. In response to the dumbfounded look on her face, I told her, "After you have seen the proof of concept demonstration that's been set up in the operations area, I'll give you the other half if my idea doesn't meet my $100 a minute cost-savings claim."

Normally, this group of executives would require you to schedule demonstrations at some other time to accommodate their perceived busy schedules, but on this particular day, they couldn't wait to see it. They were anxious to learn what was going to happen to the other half of my $100 bill. The "proof of concept" demonstration went great and I was promoted to a director position as a result of having sold my idea with some pizzazz. I also got to keep both halves of the $100 bill, and no, I don't always carry a $100 bill in my front pocket. I only do it when I want to sell something with pizzazz.

Know How to Answer the Big Question

Are you any good? Several years ago, Senator Edward Kennedy was trying to capture the Democratic Party's presidential nomination. During an interview with newsman Roger Mudd, he was asked why he wanted to become the president of the United States. He couldn't answer the question. It wasn't that he came up with a poor answer, he couldn't find any words at all. It made it seems as if he didn't have any motivation or was just going through the motions of satisfying his father's (Joe Kennedy) ambition. The public blasted him with the statement, "If he can't make a better case for himself than this, why should we vote for him? He must not be any good!" Shortly after the interview, his campaign was disbanded.

Senator Kennedy had committed the same blunder that people who are trying to promote themselves make every day. He was trying to get himself promoted, but couldn't tell anybody why he was the best man for the job. You've seen the same thing happen to your associates. They meet with their boss to tell them they deserve to be promoted because they have been with the company since the beginning of time. When the boss asks, "What have you done for me lately?" they offer the same blank stare that Kennedy gave to his interviewer. If you're trying to sell your car, would you tell a prospective buyer, "Buy this car because I'm trying to sell it"? Rather, you'd be smart to pitch all of the attractive benefits and features of your car to entice the person to buy it.

Whenever you present yourself, always be armed with facts, figures, and anything else that will support your case. Take the time to outline everything you have done for the company that justifies your promotion. Compare your accomplishments with the accomplishments of other people who may be vying for the same position. When you're all done, answer the question, "Why do you want this position?" Answers like, "I want this position because I know I can do a great job" won't cut it. A more appropriate answer might be, "I want this position because it is the focus of my career and fulfills my ambition of having the opportunity to implement my new ideas for our growing company. I've been training to do just that over the past two years and I'm the best person qualified for this position. Here's why...." Take the time to create a one-page position resume that you can hand to whomever interviews you. The reason why you want the position should be listed at the top of the resume followed by a bullet list of accomplishments that document why you are the best person qualified for the position.

Develop Your Self-Confidence

Several years ago, I discovered the important role confidence plays in the sales game. I was general manager for Computech, a small computer consulting company in Seattle that offered contract programming, computer time-sharing, and systems design services. There were only 10 of us in the company. I had been asked by the president of Cole and Weber, a well-known advertising agency, to meet with him and his executive staff to help them determine if they needed to install an in-house computer or buy time on our computer to meet their data processing needs.

The competition that I faced consisted of the mega-firms including IBM, DEC, and Hewlett Packard who all knew how to sell computer iron in the big city. As far as they were concerned, I was nothing more than a fly in the ointment that a fly swatter could eliminate. I was intimidated by the competition and the hole in my confidence was big enough to accommodate a dump truck.

Even though I enjoyed a good reputation in my field and sold enough computer services to make a nice living, there were times when I didn't get the business because I felt there was no way my micro-sized company could compete against the big guys. That's precisely where my thinking was when I was about to approach the execs at Cole and Weber. My sales plan was to make a quick presentation so that I could get out of there as quickly as possible to recover my lost confidence.

One of my associates, sensing my apprehension, told me something I never forgot: "You're not selling your company, you're selling yourself, and a solution that's right for this client, based on what you know. That puts the competition on a level playing field because it's you against the one guy from IBM, DEC, and Hewlett Packard, respectively who also have to make presentations." He was right! When I made my presentation and showed the Cole and Weber execs how much they could save by purchasing computer time from Computech rather than buying or leasing a computer, I made the sale.

As the years go by, and you're climbing further up the corporate ladder, it's easy to lose sight of the fact that you're a lot better than you may give yourself credit for. When a hole opens up in our confidence, we are often not aware of it or we try to ignore it. As a result, we may walk ploddingly down the path and lose that old bounce we once had in our step. Don't let this happen to you because if you lose the bounce, you'll stop your promotional progress. Fill the holes in your confidence level with cement as soon as you discover them and you will continue to move up instead of down the ladder.

(?) *Help:* Don Essig's book, *Motivational Minutes* (Career Press, 1997), is filled with all kinds of ideas and ways to pump your self-confidence up by using motivation.

Negotiate to Get Anything You Want

I was sitting alone at a corner table in a cafeteria a few years back, next to the window that looks out over a duck pond. My attention was focused on Steve Meiers who was sitting with some of his pals over on the other side of the room. I could tell they were all getting ready to leave and if my strategy worked, they would have to pass by my table to get at the cafeteria's exit door. I was contemplating flagging Steve down when he passed me on his way out.

Steve ran the marketing department, which was part of my dilemma. I was vice president of sales, and according to my MBA philosophy, sales and marketing are supposed to be a hand-in-glove operation. Not in this company. The marketing people think the sales people are drones because marketing has all the good ideas. Conversely, the salespeople think the marketing people are a bunch of wimps who wouldn't know what to do if they had to talk to a real customer.

This stereotype rivalry struck me as nonsense, and I suspected that Steve felt the same way. But I didn't know because I had been reluctant to approach him on the subject. And yet, I desperately needed his help on the new customer service program I was spearheading. Maybe I could negotiate a truce with Steve that would even lead to an end of the rivalry between our departments. As Steve walked by my table, I beckoned, "Steve, got a couple of minutes? I'd like to kick an idea around with you." Steve agreed to meet with me later that afternoon.

The art of negotiating can take on a formal as well as informal approach. Negotiating, if properly exploited, can be a very powerful sales tool in your promotional kit. Successful negotiating happens when you apply the exchange formula to the process. You offer to give a person something he or she wants in exchange for something you want. Returning to our previous example, I wanted Steve to share his customer service expertise with me. How did I find out what he wanted in return? I asked him! The conversation might go something like this: "Steve, I need your help and advice on what I need to do to establish a top-rate customer service department. In return, I'll offer my assistance to you in any way I can. Just tell me what you need. Can we get together this afternoon?"

? *Help:* Gerard Nierenberg is one of the world's most respected instructors in the field of negotiating, and in his eye-opening audio book, *The Art of Negotiating* (Dove Books, 1987), he helps you see why everything is negotiable. In the process, he shows you how to take advantage of that fact by applying a series of simple and proven techniques. When you finish the book, you will know how to negotiate.

Play the Power Sales Game

Have you ever discovered that the promotion you expected had been awarded to someone else? Was the reason you lost out because of your incompetence in a critical area, a poor interview, seniority, or because someone didn't like you? The most likely reason why you didn't get promoted was probably because you competitor made all of the right moves and knew how to play the power sales game better than you did. The effective use of power at the appropriate time can make all of the difference in who wins the sale, or promotion in this case, and who loses. The sidelines are covered with losers who are always saying, "If that's the way the game is played, then I'm not going to play." If you don't play the game, you'll never win.

If you want to be successful at playing the power sales game, watch how the masters do it. Masters recognize power's manifestations and know when and how to apply it in every aspect of their professional life. For them, every human encounter offers them an opportunity to test their power playing capabilities. They play the game 24 hours a day as they spar with everyone from parking lot attendants to their peers and superiors, instinctively trying to control every situation to their advantage.

They'll even use ordinary human encounters for practice. Some of the best power players I know develop many of their techniques at swap meets negotiating bargain prices as a means of studying human emotion such as resistance under pressure, feigned hesitation, and compromise. The trick is to develop a power style you're comfortable with that fits your character and personality. Fine tune your own way to play the power sales game by developing power techniques that will help you get promoted. Following are several basic moves to consider.

Know when to play a weakness. Most people believe that power players should always display strengths and never show any signs of weakness. Games of weakness are underestimated, particularly by men who are eager to display their macho personalities. If you need more funding for a major project, it may be appropriate to call attention to the fact that the project will die if your funding request is denied. Remember it's the squeaky wheel that always gets the grease.

Avoid victories over superiors. Suppose your boss invites you to an important presentation with the company's president to win approval on her desire to consolidate two departments. As you listen to the presentation, she makes a number of statements that you know for a fact, are not true. Somehow, you manage to keep your mouth shut. At the end of the presentation, the president looks at you and asks for your opinion. You have two clear choices to make. You can use this situation as an opportunity to exploit power over your boss and tell the president what's wrong with the presentation. Or you can play it safe and avoid cutting your own throat by saying, "I agree with everything my boss had to say on the proposed consolidation." Only on very rare occasions does it pay to exploit power over a superior.

Make decisions you can't make. Sometimes it's appropriate to pretend you have autonomous and unlimited decision-making authority, even when you don't have it. For example, you're in a meeting and asked by the group to make a decision that you know must first be approved by your boss. The powerless statement to make is, "Gee, I'll first have to ask my boss if it's okay." The far more powerful approach would be to say, "I'll think about it and make my decision later on today." That gives you time to check in with the boss and leads everyone to believe that you are still the primary decision-maker.

Use personal humiliation as an effective weapon. Counter any complaint or difficult request with your own problems to offset the situation. For example, when one of your peers confronts you with a problem you don't want to address, just say, "I would love to talk to you about it, but if you could see my calendar, you wouldn't believe it. I know you need more money but things are tough on all of us." Playing the humiliation game requires you to sigh a lot, hold your head in your hands, and always carry a look of extreme weariness.

Apply information power. Everybody is dependent on a supply of information to make decisions. And yet, we'll spend hours in meetings discussing major questions of policy or direction without relying on factual information to help in the decision-making process. Have you ever been in a meeting when someone finally say, "Based on the information I have accumulated, I think we should do the following..."? Just the word "information" brings a hush to the room as everybody turns to listen to what the newfound "expert" with the information has to say. Good power players know when and how to use information to get their way.

These are just a couple of ways to play the power sales game. There's a whole universe of possibilities and combinations available to individual power players. Always remember that you must consistently keep yourself in a controlled power position to assure your promotion. Controlled power means that you know exactly what you are doing and how you are exercising your power in any situation. Avoid large outbursts of uncontrolled power such as becoming irate, which can cause you irreparable harm.

? *Help:* Michael Korda wrote an excellent book about power and how to use it to get ahead. It was appropriately titled *Power!* (Random House, 1991). It's must reading for anybody who wants to learn more about how to strategically play the power sales game. Although the book is out of print, I found the book in a good public library.

Use Winning Sales Tactics

What do you do if you're confronted by someone who knows how to play the sales game better than you do? What are some of the tactics they'll use and how can you neutralize them with your own tactics? If you know how to recognize certain sales tactics, or conversely, weakness signals that people give off, you'll be in a much better position to take advantage of the situation. Here's how:

Foot tactics. The bottom of one's foot is a sensitive part of the body. Most people will only expose the soles of their shoes when they feel they are in a protected position and are comfortable. Watch an executive in action at a meeting making a presentation to sell a controversial idea to the group. He or she will sit back, one leg crossed over the other in a display of self-assurance that shows they are in control. The moment the discussion turns serious and they're challenged with tough questions, watch them suddenly uncross their legs, lean forward, and place both feet firmly on the ground in an attempt to hold their position. At this point, they subconsciously feel vulnerable and the person addressing them has two choices: Do the same thing to the point where both of you are hunched over in a mutual combat position, or lean back and cross your legs, expressing indifference and a lack of fear at the other's power stance.

Swing tactics. Other ways feet give away a person's power stance is when they swing their feet back and forth to indicate impatience or doubt. If you see a person suddenly pull their feet back so they're out of sight under their chair, the person is afraid or concerned about something that was just said. Feet that are solidly placed in front of a person you're addressing are an indication that this person is not willing to compromise.

Desk tactics. Analyzing a person's desk can help you determine their personality style. If they're an insecure person, they will sit behind a huge wooden desk that acts as their barricade. It's always easier to sell your idea with these types if you can tempt them out from behind their fortress and get them to sit on a sofa or chair in an open area. Ask them to join you for lunch or for coffee in the cafeteria. If you can't get them to move out from behind their big desk, put your briefcase on their desk before you start talking to them, which will make them nervous because you will have infringed upon their protective space. It's the only way you can disrupt their secure position. When they are in that position, they're much more prone to give you "no" answers than "yes" answers.

Phone tactics. The best way to play the telephone tactic game is to have the ability to place any outbound call whenever your want and only accept the inbound calls you want. When your inbound calls are less than your outbound calls, there's a loss of power because it's an indication fewer people want to talk to you. If that happens, take corrective steps to boost your inbound call volume. When you run into someone in the hallway who wants to meet with you to discus some issue, even if you have your Daytimer in your front pocket, tell them, "Call me and I'll check my schedule" or better yet, "Call my secretary to schedule a time."

Paging tactics. The controlled use of paging can do wonders to show people how important you really are. I know of several successful people who routinely have their secretaries or associates call them wherever they're having a business lunch in an attempt to impress their guest. This technique works even better when you're at a company social function and you want everybody to know that you're there.

Office space tactics. A large office is pointless unless it is arranged so that anybody who comes into your office has to walk the maximum number of steps to get to your desk. Even if you have a relatively small office, you can still accomplish this feat by placing as many obstacles as possible in the path of anybody entering your office. Coffee tables, chairs, sofas, for example can all serve the purpose of exploiting the size of your office. Remember, the bigger your office, the more tactical power you have. Regardless of your office size, always have the visitor's chairs facing toward you so that you're separated from them by the width of the desk to pre-serve your tactical position. If the back of your desk chair faces a wall, allow yourself plenty of room to roll your chair back from your desk if you want to create more space between you and an office visitor.

Time tactics. The effective use of time is one of the ultimate ways to display authority, even when you don't have it. Whoever controls time controls the situation in most instances. Time players will always remind anyone who wants to meet with them that their time is valuable. However, there may be situations where you will want to reverse your use of tight time tactics. Let's say you have agreed to meet with one of your peers to discuss a difficult situation that has developed between your two respective depart-ments. You need more help from your peer than she needs from you to get things resolved, even though you've told her your time is limited. When she enters your office at the appointed hour, take your watch off ostentatiously, and place it face down on your desk. Say, "My time belongs to you for as long as you need it." Watch the cooperation level of your peer go up exponentially at the outset of your meeting. You'll be able to get anything you want from her. Al-ternatively, taking your watch off and placing it face up on your desk without saying a word announces to your visitor that they had better make their point in short order because you haven't got much time.

Busy tactics. The busier you can make yourself look to others, the more you can impose your schedule on them to improve your tactical position. One way to accomplish this is to schedule a meeting and publish a schedule showing people when they will make their respective presentations. Let them know they'll be called just before their time comes up. Look what you will have ac-complished from a power perspective. You are now controlling the schedule of several individuals who are forced to remain in their offices close to their phones waiting to receive your important phone call.

The desire to always be in control of any given situation should be one of your most basic objectives in your drive to get yourself promoted. In this section, I've introduced several tactics that you can use to control events in your own best interest. If you can do that on a consistent basis, your self-confidence and your ability to sell your ideas to others will go up exponentially.

(?) *Help:* *Superstar Sales Secrets* (Career Press, 1995) by Barry Farber contains every key question you should be prepared to ask when you are trying to sell something. It's a great guidebook for anyone who is not familiar with basic sales techniques.

Idea: In power sales, like in war, there is no substitute for victory. Always remember that selling your ideas is a little like wrestling a gorilla. You don't quit when you are tired. You quit when the gorilla is tired.

Make Great First Impressions

You never get a second chance to make a good first impression. You make first impressions every day and you succeed or fail by the impressions you create in briefings, interviews, phone calls, meetings, and a myriad of other daily encounters. In today's fast paced work environment, deals are won or lost, careers are made or destroyed, relationships are established or broken, all in a matter of minutes based upon first impressions.

Research shows that lasting first impressions are formed in as little as four minutes or less. If you fail to make a good first impression in the allotted time frame, it becomes much more difficult, if not impossible, to sell, persuade, or influence anyone to accept your way of thinking. Those first four minutes can make or break your dreams of promotion. According to the psychology community, more than 90 percent of the impressions we convey have nothing to do with what we actually say. More than half of our first meeting with someone is communicated nonverbally—by how we look. Most of the rest of our meaning is conveyed by how we sound. Only a small percentage depends on the content of our actual message.

First impressions are made up of the things people notice about you during the first few minutes they meet you. They include your appearance, facial expressions, movement, your tone of voice, and the words you use, as well as a variety of other data that helps them form their first impression of you. If their first impression is positive, you can generally count on their support. If the impression is negative, you will have difficulty dealing with them and it may be impossible to change their opinion.

Promotions are awarded to those who know how to make lasting, good first impressions—from the manager who's trying to sell his budget to the executive committee to the salesman who's trying to close a sale. In fact, you may not realize how much of your average day is spent making first impressions. On average, you'll spend 85 percent of your day in some form of communication (that is, speaking, listening, or writing).

The typical worker will make between 10 and 12 speeches per year including presentations to staffs, peers, superiors, community groups, and professional associations.

Most of us spend more time on the telephone than we do on our personal computers.

According to *Harvard Business Review*, communication skills rate second only to job knowledge as important factors in a person's success.

? *Help:* How can you win in a business deal if the other person has their own personal agenda? You do it by making a great first impression. Gerard Nierenberg shows you how in his book, *How to Read a Person Like a Book* (Pocket Books, 1982). He shows you how to interpret body language, detect lies, improve your negotiating skills, and take command of the situation.

Warning: All of us make important first impressions every day whether we're meeting with clients, our bosses, colleagues, or employees to discuss our ideas or to negotiate a deal. If you make a good first impression, you will frame a positive response from whomever you're communicating with and favorably sustain your promotional objectives. If you fail to make a good first impression, you'll be hard pressed to get an opportunity to reinstate yourself with a second chance.

Know How to Sell Your Ideas

The powerful art of persuading others that your ideas are great and should therefore be implemented is critical to the promotional process. The more ideas you sell, the more people will think of you as a contributor to the organization. Here are five great techniques you can use whenever you're trying to sell someone on your ideas:

1. Always stress benefits. If you want sell your ideas, never suggest an action without stating its benefit. Suppose you say to your boss, "I need to take over the Harding project." That's the idea you want to sell but you haven't offered him the benefit part of the equation. You add, "I can then leverage my excellent relationship with Mr. Harding to get this project back on the right track. Mr. Harding will work with me to find an acceptable solution." Before you attempt to sell any idea, think about all of the benefits that you can bring to the table, and suggest them in their sequence of importance. Save your best for the last and only use them if needed.

2. Explore reasons of disagreement. When people disagree with you, explore the reasons for their objection. It's one of the most difficult sales tactics to apply, but it's the one that can offer you the biggest payback. We all have a natural tendency to jump into a conversation and offer an immediate answer to an objection just to get it out of the way. The problem is that the person making the objection may not be listening after they stated their objection.

They're thinking about what else they can say to buttress their objection. To get them to link their thinking with yours, ask them a question about their objection so that you understand exactly why they made the objection. You have to inquire into their reasoning. Suppose you're trying to sell someone on a new time-saving way to do their job and they reply with, "That's too complicated." How can you counter his objection without knowing what they mean by "complicated"? Another advantage of inquiring into an objection is that you're showing interest in their objection. Questions are powerful, versatile sales tools. Use them whenever you can.

3. Explain why when asking a question. Whenever you ask a question, say why you're asking it. If a question stands alone, it raises another question in the listeners mind, like, "Why did he ask that question?" The person you're talking to will instantly stop listening to you as they contemplate possible answers in their mind. They can become irritated if they don't know why you're asking the question. They might feel like you are cross-examining them or they may feel anxious because your question is a demand on them to provide you with information. You can eliminate these problems if, for example, you precede your question with, "Let me ask you a question to make sure I understand what you just said." In addition to possibly jumping to the wrong conclusion about what someone has said, you show an interest in what the person is communicating to you, which in turn sharpens their listening powers in what you have to say.

4. Justify your conclusions. When you make a concluding statement, state why you think it is appropriate. If you give the basis of your conclusion, you'll greatly increase your credibility. Recognize that some people are skeptical if they don't know how you drew your conclusions and may subsequently believe that you don't know what you're talking about. To negate the problem, you might say, "Based on the numbers I have shown you, I believe that it would be appropriate to implement my idea. What do you think?" By adding the "What do you think" question, you offer the person an opportunity to either agree or disagree with the basis of your conclusion. If they disagree, at least you have gained the sales advantage of knowing they have an objection so that you can respond accordingly.

5. *Back up your sales pitch.* When you attempt to persuade someone to accept your idea, you may need to provide information to back up your claims. That can be a challenge because you typically don't know what question they will ask that demands supporting data. Unfortunately, just one broken link in the reasoning chain can take away the support of all the good links you've built in it. Even if your sales case doesn't collapse, it can weaken your effectiveness. Anticipate the types of questions you will be asked and the support data you'll need to avoid this problem. Ask you colleagues who have critically oriented minds to help you out by asking you question in advance of your presentation.

? *Help:* If you are interested in learning more about how to sell your ideas, read *How to Get Your Point Across in 30 Seconds* (Washington Square Press, 1991) by Milo Frank. It's must reading for anybody who is trying to get promoted. If you can master the art of consistently getting your point across in a matter of seconds, you are on your way.

Ask the Right Questions

Questions are one of the most powerful selling tools you can use, and yet people are reluctant to ask questions when they are in a selling situation. Perhaps it's because they feel that by asking a question, they're displaying their ignorance. And you can only ask so many questions before you begin to irritate the other person. You have to be assertive to ask questions. If you're not an assertive person, it may be difficult for you to ask questions. In spite of the perceived drawbacks of asking questions, it's the most rewarding part of selling yourself. It requires quick thinking, keen listening capabilities, and organized thoughts to reap the benefits that you'll get from the answers to carefully worded questions. Here are several ways asking questions can help you sell yourself and your ideas:

Diagnosing objections. When you attempt to sell anything such as an idea, you need to reduce the natural resistance the other person will have to whatever it is you're trying to sell. When they raise objections, you are obligated to respond, but you do that only after you understand the line of reasoning that's behind their objection. You're trying to answer the question, "How did they come up with the reasoning behind the objection?" When somebody disagrees with you, their objection is symptomatic of the fact that their thinking may not line up with your thinking. You've got to diagnose what caused the problem before you can render a solution. One of the best ways to do that is to ask questions to uncover the other person's reasoning to see where they are coming from.

Loose objections. As the name implies, a loose objection is one that's based on loose or no facts, which can make them difficult to diagnose. Suppose the person your talking to tells you they don't like your idea because someone they know says it won't work. You now have to move to questions that will get them to reason along with you by asking, "Have they ever tried to implement my idea? What kind of expertise do they have that's relative to my idea? Did they give me specifics as to why it won't work?" Once you find the weak points that are inherent in the objection, you can exploit the appropriate reasoning as to why the objection is not valid.

Gain insight. Asking questions is the best way there is to gain insight and information that you need to strengthen your sales presentation. Questions can also be used to help the other person gain insight into your way of thinking, which should be one of your sales objectives. Suppose you're trying to sell a cost-cutting idea. Before you present the specifics of your idea, you might ask, "Jim, do you believe that prudent cost cutting is critical to our organization right now?" If you get a "yes" answer, you are ready to introduce your cost-cutting idea. If you elicit a "no" response, you had better find out why Jim feels this way before you proceed with your idea.

Adjusting questions. Think of the question as an adjustable sales tool. You can use wide-open questions to get a broad range of information or you can ask questions to pinpoint the facts that you want. Using questions with various settings will help you sell yourself by getting exactly what you want or for guiding the other person's thinking so that it's in line with yours. An example of a wide-open question would be, "What do you think?" A narrow question might be, "Do you agree?" In-between questions might ask for a number, a reason, an opinion, or an explanation.

Introduction questions. Another kind of question to ask is one that introduces information that the other person may not have considered. These types of questions can be used very effectively to change the direction of the other person's thinking. You might start an introduction question with, "What if I could show you imperial numbers that would prove my point. Would that change your mind?" If you extract a "yes" response, you can then present numbers for your listener to review. Other ways to phrase this type of question are to ask, "Did you know that...?" or "What do you now think?"

Raised questions. Whenever you ask a question, it may raise another question like, "Why are you asking me that question?" It's human nature to be suspicious and some people want to know your reasoning before they will provide you with an answer. Whenever you ask a question, follow up with, "The reason why I asked is because I need more information." This clarifies why you're asking a question without getting into an elaborate explanation.

As a general rule, it's best not to ask a question unless you know why you're asking it. if you can't do this, then chances are the question isn't worth asking. Work out where you want to go with your questions before you ask them. Think of questions as sales tools you can use to help people think straight and to make the best decision.

(?) *Help:* Jesse Nirenberg's book, *How to Sell Your Ideas* (McGraw-Hill, 1991), offers some excellent advice on a variety of techniques that you can use to sell your ideas to your subordinates, your peers, your boss, and upper management by asking the right question.

Add Value to Everything You Do

It's essential that you come across as a "value adder" to the higher-ups in your company if you want to get promoted. Nobody gets promoted to any meaningful position if they are not capable of adding value to their organizations. If you're in sales, the value you add to the organization is relatively easy to measure. How many new accounts did you add and how much did you increase sales this year over last year are two important value-added components. If the numbers are favorable, you get promoted. What about the rest of you who are not in sales positions where value may not be as easy to measure? How do you add value to your organizations so that your accomplishments get recognized and you're rewarded with a promotion?

Unfortunately, value has different meanings to different people. You may add value by doing something for your organization that may not even register with the top execs. Maybe you have identified a way to reduce the cost of packaging that will save the company several thousands of dollars a year. Sure, you get a nice cash reward and a plastic plaque to hang on your wall. If the exec or manager who is ultimately responsible for making your promotion a reality doesn't care, then enjoy your plaque because that's all you'll get!

In all fairness to the exec in our example, he or she may not care about the cost-savings program you implemented because it's way down on their list of priorities. They may be more concerned about a presentation they will be making next week because the charts that they have developed stink. Suppose they, their secretary, or someone divulged that concern to you. You picked up on the opportunity, approached the exec, and offered to refine their presentation charts. They took you up on your offer and you subsequently produced a set of charts that dazzled everybody at their presentation. Now, you have added value and struck gold at the same time. Guess who this exec will call on to help them prepare for their next presentation? You, of course.

The moral of the story is to never assume that whatever you're doing automatically helps you get promoted. If you believe that it adds self-anointed value, that's great in that it provides you with a sense of accomplishment. And while that is certainly a noble achievement, does it also add recognized value?

Warning: If you don't aim higher, you'll never go higher. High jumpers are always raising the bar to see if they can clear the new height they set for themselves. Inevitably, they won't clear the bar on the first jump, but over time and with lots of practice, they will make the jump successfully. Learn to expect more of yourself. Raise the bar and set new standards that tell people what you can be counted on to do. Review your productivity level, the quality of your work, and how often you take the initiative as starting points. Create new, more efficient ways of doing things, double check your work to avoid errors, or volunteer to do something each week that nobody else wants to do.

Use Visualization

Visualization is a powerful tool that you can use to mentally prepare yourself to perform at peak levels under pressure. It will help you feel more confident and in control when you enter any new or challenging situation, like trying to sell yourself in front of a large audience. By utilizing visualization to harness the incredible power of your imagination, you'll be amazed at what you will be able to accomplish. You'll find yourself performing at levels that you never thought were possible.

Before you go into any pressure-filled situation, allow your mind to set a positive image of what you want to accomplish. Focus not only on what you want to happen but what you don't want to happen as well. Then, see yourself accomplishing your goal. Visualizing success is a technique that many top sports champions use.

Golf's legendary Jack Nicklaus is a prime example. He attributes 10 percent of his success to his setup before the shot, 40 percent to his stance and swing, and 50 percent to his mental imagery of the shot. "I never hit a shot, not even in practice, without having a sharp, in-focus picture of the shot in my mind before I take it," he said. He imagines his swing, the ball in flight, and where it will land. It usually lands exactly where he thought it would.

Having a positive mental picture of what you want to accomplish will help you create the corresponding behavior. Visualization will not only help you direct your personal performance but it will help you validate new processes as well. Use it to check out a new product or program you're developing, as you run through the implementation processes mentally from start to finish to make sure you've thought of everything. It can help you ascertain if there are any problems you may have missed. If you're developing a strategy to sell an idea to your boss, visualize yourself *as your boss* to anticipate his or her wants and needs. If you're about to make a presentation to a large group, what do they want to hear?

Dick Munro, the former CEO of Time-Warner says that as part of his preparation for an important speech, he visualizes the environment surrounding the presentation. "I'll see in my mind what the room looks like, who will be there, how they will be seated, and how I want to come across." If you do the same thing and always visualize yourself as a winner, you will be much better prepared to handle any situation.

● *Warning:* If the blind lead the blind, both shall fall into the ditch. A successful presenter must take the lead in everything they say and do. Do not let your audience lead you.

Look and Sound Great

Although we spend nearly every waking moment talking or listening to someone, the truth of the matter is that most of us don't have the faintest notion of what we look like to others, how we sound, or even what we say. In the initial stages of a conversation, what you look like can be as important as how you say something. It's during the first few minutes of interaction with others that their attention span is at its greatest, their eyes and ears are focused on you as they form a first impression. If their impression is favorable, they'll continue listening to what you have to say. If it's unfavorable, they will either stop listening or come up with an excuse to end the conversation. You'll never sell yourself and your ideas effectively if you make an unfavorable first impression. Here are several issues to consider when you attempt to make a good first impression:

Dress to blend. Have you ever heard the expression, "Make sure you dress the part?" Although there certainty are aspects of our appearance that we can't change like our race, sex, or age, we can control certain aspects of our appearance to improve our odds of making a favorable first impression. As a general rule of thumb, you are on safer grounds if you dress to blend in with the people you are addressing. If you're attending a meeting and you are the only one wearing a three-piece suit when everyone else is dressed casual, you will stand out. It could cause your audience to become suspicious. "Why is this guy all dressed up? Does he think he's better than the rest of us?" Those are not what you want people to think when they start to form a first impression.

What do you sound like? Your voice tells a lot about your personality, attitude, and anxiety level. What you sound like can have big payoffs in situations such as job interviews, presentations, or confrontations. If you can learn to recognize signs of tension and stress in your voice and the voices of others, you can take steps to tune your voice to a more appropriate level for a given situation. You can also adjust your voice accordingly when someone you're talking to divulges their position as a result of their voice. Through the analysis of your own voice and the voices of others, you will learn which aspects of your voice you want to work on and which ones you would leave alone.

What do you say? You can enhance and exploit an initial positive impression if you communicate effectively. To do this, you must know what to say and how you say it. In the movie *Consolidated Brands*, Howard Bergman was a CEO who wanted to improve the company's customer relations image. When a group of angry customers camped outside his office, he surprised them by opening the door, and invited them into his office. Bergman shook hands with each person, asked their names, and worked the crowd in his charismatic style. He then motioned for everybody to sit down, and as they began taking their places, he perched himself on the edge of his desk. As he waited patiently for everybody to be seated, he looked directly at each person in the room. Finally, he opened his suit jacket and began speaking in a friendly but strong voice. "I understand you have some concerns about one of our new products and I'd like to hear them." Bergman's style was a good example of a balance between what is said and how it is said.

All three channels of information (body, voice, and words) need to work in harmony to assure you'll make a favorable first impression. This matter of balance between language and delivery is critical. If one channel is out of sync with another, a double message may be communicated leaving the person who's listening to figure out what you look like or how you say it. Most of the time, they'll believe your body language and tone of voice over what words you say. Your actions truly speak louder than your words.

? *Help: The Body Language Workbook* (New Harbinger Press, 1995) by Thomas Cash includes a seven-step program for learning how to shape what you look like with body language.

Don't Get Stressed

Trying to sell anything can be a stressful experience. If you're stressed out when you make a presentation, you'll tighten up, you'll feel tense, and your sales presentation will suffer accordingly. Several years ago, sports psychologists believed that athletes needed to experience extreme tension to get their flow of adrenaline going in order to perform well. They're now finding that relaxation improves an athlete's performance far better than stress.

We have all experienced different aspects of stress when we've tried to persuade others to do something. Stress starts to occur when the other person objects to something you've just said. The hairs on the back of your neck start to rise and you become tense. As a result, the tension disrupts your reasoning and blocks your rational responsiveness to what your audience is saying. Instead of exercising self-control and sensitive reasoning that's needed to win someone over to your way of thinking, you start to attack with counter arguments that will inevitably prevent you from selling your original idea.

Force yourself to relax before you enter into any stressful conversation. Close your eyes and concentrate on your breathing for about a minute. Lean back in your chair, put your feet on the desk, clasp your hands, think of a happy thought, and smile. Then repeat to yourself as many times as necessary, "I will not let my emotions adversely control this conversation." If you can't relax, postpone the discussion.

Another way to control stress is to take the position that nothing in your mind is finalized. Your idea looks good to you, but you have to hear what others think before you can determine if it's really a good idea. There may be good reasons why your idea will not work. You'll find out if you give credit to objections people present to you and inquire with questions to solicit their thoughts in a non-stressful manner.

If you maintain an attitude of trying to make the right decision, even if it goes against your idea, you'll avoid the worst thing that can happen to you when you try to sell yourself—becoming an adversary. Nobody ever sells their ideas when they are in an adversarial stance. When you become an adversary, you automatically force the other person to become one as well. The end result is that both of you will be so busy thinking about what you're going to say next to block each other's objections that your original idea will be lost in the confrontation.

Adversaries don't think objectively about each other. They don't inquire into each other's reasoning to see if the other has something to offer that would benefit them. If you want to sell your ideas, to control your stress, psyche yourself up before you engage in a conversation. You've got to be willing to accept a course of objectively examining the other person's position and comparing it with yours. Constantly remind yourself to resist the impulse of pounding away with words to make your case without listening to what the other person has to say.

(?) *Help: 60 Second Stress Management* (New Horizon Press, 1991) by Dr. Andrew Goliszek shows you how to control your stress anytime by applying a simple but proven set of stress-eliminating exercises.

Master the Art of Persuasion

Have you ever caught yourself saying, "That idiot doesn't know what I'm trying to tell him. How am I ever going to get him accept my idea?" Becoming an effective and persuasive communicator will solve the problem every time. It also fulfills a critical need that you must learn to master if you want to get promoted. Before we talk about what you can do to become a master persuader, let's first make sure we have a clear understanding of the difference between persuasion and manipulation. Although many people think that persuasion is just a kinder word for manipulation, there's a huge difference between the two terms.

According to Webster's, manipulation is the act of using any means necessary to force a person to do something that fulfills your needs, whether or not it's in their best interest. Conversely, persuasion is the art of guiding someone through a logical progression of thoughts so that they can arrive at a conclusion that complements your views and is also in their own best interest. In essence, persuasion enables the other person to understand what you are saying, what you are feeling, and consequently become motivated to do what you initially believed was in their best interest.

A classic example of persuasion occurred when I was attending army boot camp and was talking to my buddy while one of the sergeants was conducting a class on land mines. He abruptly interrupted our conversation and said, "You better listen to what I'm telling you, boy, because it could save your life." From that point on, I was all ears because he had persuaded me with a hook: my life. In the business world, you are constantly challenged to get people to do things you want them to do. If you're the boss, you can apply manipulative tactics when you tell a subordinate, "Here's a task I want you to do. Don't ask any questions. Just do it." Or you can apply persuasive tactics like, "Here's a task I'd like you to do. Before you get started, let's first discuss why it's important to you and our organization." Leaders persuade with hooks. Idiots manipulate with force.

There are three basic types of hooks that you can use to persuade people to do anything you want. The personal hook is one of the most effective hooks you can use. The sergeant used my life as a personal hook to persuade me to listen. Name-dropping can be another effective personal reference hook. Suppose you're trying to get an appointment with a vice president who can influence your promotional opportunities. She doesn't know you from Adam, which is one of the reasons why you need to see her. One of the guys in your network know her well and recommended that you meet her. You persuade her to see you when you say, "A mutual associate of ours, Dave Rye, suggested that I give you a call and set up a half-hour meeting with you. Would 10 a.m. tomorrow work for you?"

The second persuasive hook is a question. To be effective, the question must be very specific so that the listener must think carefully before responding. The purpose of the question hook is to take the listener's mind off whatever they were doing before you asked the question and to provide you with information you can use to persuade them to do something. Let's say you have a great idea on how to promote a new product your company is about to introduce. Somehow, you need to persuade the vice president of marketing to accept your idea, which would a great feather in your hat. You approach him and ask, "What do you think about the new product we're introducing next month?"

The question gets your listeners to focus their thoughts on the new product and subsequently opens the door for you to discuss your product introduction ideas. When you listen to their response, you may pick up valuable information that could help you persuade them. Suppose he says, "It's a great product, but quite frankly, we are having a tough time figuring out how we're going to introduce it." You just hit pay dirt and you're on your way when you say, "I've got a great product introduction idea for you to consider."

The third persuasive hook uses a strong statement. Here's an example: You walk into your boss's office for your appointed meeting, shut the door, and say, "If we don't take some immediate action, we're going to lose our largest account. I have several ideas that will prevent that from happening." In one hook statement, you have captured your boss's focused attention on the problem and his interest in learning about your solutions.

All three hooks, when used in combination, can be powerful tools in persuading someone to do something you want them to do. Jane Fonda used all three hooks in her fitness video commercials, which went something like this: "Hi, I'm Jane Fonda and I have an important message for you (personal hook). Are you one of the 50 million Americans who try to lose weight each year (question hook)? Diets simply don't work as you'll learn when you order my tape (strong statement hook)." That 15-second commercial per-suaded millions of people to run out and buy Jane's fitness video.

Your effective use of hooks when you initiate a conversation will get your listener to focus on what you have to say. There's one final element of persuasion that you should also consider. How do you get the person to take action in your favor? Every person has a desire for gain and if they perceive that they will gain some-thing by following your persuasive lines of thought, they'll take ac-tion. In Jane Fonda's case, she offered her listeners a free copy of her fitness book if they ordered her video within a specified time frame, which is an example of a material goods gain. Personal gain can take other forms including security, acceptance, success, and wealth.

A person's innate fear of loss can also be effectively used to per-suade a person to act in your favor. Your boss didn't want to face the consequences if his department was responsible for losing the company's largest customer so he was poised to act if you offered him a viable solution to the problem. The fear of loss has to be something that's important to your listeners before they will take action.

In conclusion, let's review the key points you need to consider to persuade people to take action.

Create an opening to your presentation using all three hooks whenever possible. Make sure everything in your presentation treats your listener with respect. Avoid making any condescending remarks. Identify all of the benefits of your idea and how it fulfils the needs of your listeners. Focus on your listener's two greatest internal motivating factors, their desire for gain and their fear of loss. List every possible objection your listener could pose to your idea and state how you will overcome each objection.

? *Help: State of the Art Selling* (Career Press, 1994) by Barry Farber is a compilation from 100 top sales performers who share the sales secrets that have led to their success.

Chapter 4

Motivating Yourself

Have you ever seen a motivational speaker work a group of people up into a state of cheering, yelling, and arm-waving hysteria? The really good ones brim over with self-confidence as they assure their audience that if people really believe in themselves, they can aspire to become anything they want to be. Of course, because we all believe in ourselves, we're convinced that we too can start accomplishing miracles as soon as we get out of the seminar. With many motivational speakers, their spellbinding delivery often gets much more attention than their words.

Inspirational speakers play on our emotions, and are experts at getting our pulse pounding and our adrenaline racing, which is why people pay big bucks to see their "performances." However, their speeches are useless if your intent in seeing one goes beyond entertainment, like boosting your motivation. When the presentation ends, you'll jump up with the rest of the audience and get caught up in the temporary mass hysteria. Fifteen minutes after the seminar is over and you head back into the real world, you'll quickly return to normality, which is precisely where the problem lies. Your brief encounter with the motivational hype begins to dissipate in a matter of hours after the seminar.

You need to find a way to keep *yourself* motivated throughout the day, day after day as you continuously work your promotional plan. People who feel good about themselves and their prospects for a promotion consistently produce good results and inspire everyone they touch to look at them favorably. The greatest motivational challenge you have as you maneuver your way up the corporate ladder is keeping yourself motivated, even under adverse conditions.

6 Ways to Keep Yourself Motivated

All people possess a common set of needs and wants that, when triggered, activate their respective levels of motivation and their drive to improve upon their current situation. There are six motivational premises that you can apply to bolster your motivation and your chances of getting promoted.

1. You must have reasons for what you want to do. Okay, you want to get yourself promoted. Does the challenge of getting yourself promoted really turn you on? Is it something that you want to do? If your answer is no then you'll lack the motivation to get yourself promoted.

2. You must have goals and objectives that you're constantly sorting through and working on every day of the week. Your challenge is to pursue goals that fit within your plan to get yourself promoted.

3. Your behavior should be directed at goals you believe are good for you, goals that have perceived values for you. You'll lose your motivation if you pursue goals that have no personal value.

4. You should not work toward accomplishing a goal unless you believe it is attainable. Most people, no matter how valuable a goal might be to them, won't make the effort to go after it unless they believe that their chances of obtaining it are good. For example, you may fantasize about becoming the company's president, but won't do anything about it if you believe that your education is inadequate to reach that goal.

5. The situation under which a goal is pursued can change its value. The work environment can change the value of goals you're working on. For example, your boss has told you that if you reach a specific goal, you will be promoted to branch manager. When you reach your goal and discover that you will be branch manager in a remote location, the goal may lose its value to you.

6. You will only pursue goals if you are motivated, and the reverse is true: If you do not have goals to pursue, you won't be motivated.

As you apply the motivational techniques discussed in this section, observe what motivates people you admire so that you, too, can sharpen your own motivational skills. Observe their voice inflections, speaking manner, eye contact, facial expressions, posture, and self-confidence. A totally motivated person motivates not only themselves, but everyone they touch. If you can instill this practice in yourself, you'll be amazed at how much more productive you'll become, how easy it will be to get others to help you, and how totally motivated you'll become in the process.

Warning: Keep improving yourself. Everybody in today's business world could be more successful, make more money, and be happier if they really wanted to. Why, then, are so many unable to accomplish this? Somewhere along the line, they have stopped self-improving. They have become complacent and aren't willing to take the initiative to improve on what they are doing. Even more important, they are not willing to learn how to do new things that will increase their value to their organizations and themselves.

Help: If you are interested in learning more about how to motivate yourself, obtain a copy of my book *1,001 Ways to Inspire Your Organization, Your Team, and Yourself* (Career Press, 1997). If you're looking for additional ways to motivate yourself, read

Steve Chandler's book *100 Ways to Motivate Yourself* (Career Press, 1996).

Always Think Like a Winner

Keeping score is a basic necessity in our competitive society, whether it be in a baseball game or in a corporate game. In this section, I offer a number of "one liners" on what it takes to be a winner, how to increase your personal image, improve your human relationships, and drive your motivation. Although I recognize that winning is serious business in the promotional game, I felt that it was in order to introduce a humorous side to the challenge. It's my belief that we all must have the ability to sit back and laugh at ourselves in the interest of preserving our sanity as we climb up the corporate ladder.

1. A winner makes commitments and keeps them. A loser makes promises and forgets them.
2. When a winner makes a mistake, he admits it and corrects the problem. When a loser makes a mistake, he says, "It wasn't my fault" and walks off.
3. A winner works harder than a loser, but has more free time because a loser is always too busy doing nothing.
4. A winner goes through a problem to solve it, while losers go around it.
5. Winners show they're sorry when they make a mistake by making up for it, while losers say, "I'm sorry," and make the same mistake again.
6. Winners listen before they speak. Losers just wait for their turn to say something without hearing anything that was said.
7. A winner says, "There ought to be a better way." A loser says, "Why change the way we have always done it?"
8. A winner respects and tries to learn from those who know more than they do. Losers resent those who know

more than they do and will criticize them behind their backs.

9. A winner only knows one speed: fast! Losers don't have to pace themselves because they only have two speeds: slow and stop.

10. Winners have a realistic appreciation of their strengths and weaknesses. Losers are oblivious to any of their strengths or weaknesses.

11. Winners are sensitive to the feelings of others. Losers are sensitive only to their own feelings.

12. Winners give more than they get because they are always building for the future. Losers lean on those who are stronger than they are and take their frustrations out on those who are weaker than themselves.

13. Winners admit to their prejudices and are constantly working to correct them. Losers don't know how to correct anything.

14. Winners know when to stop talking after they have made their point or closed the sale. Losers keep on talking because they never know when they have made any points.

15. Winners act the same toward those who can be helpful and those who can be of no immediate help because they may be able to count on them next time. Losers ignore anyone who can't be of immediate help to them.

16. Winners know they can never stop learning even when others consider them the experts. Losers think they already know everything.

17. The saving grace of winners is their ability to laugh at themselves in a non-demeaning manner. Losers only know how to laugh at others.

18. Winners are sympathetic to weaknesses in others because they understand their own weaknesses. Losers won't recognize any of their weaknesses.

19. Winners know that in order to win, you have to be willing to give more than you take. Losers always take more than they give, even if it means stealing.

Success and failure touch on a wide variety of human endeavors that include personal self-image, values, motivation, and personal relationships. Even though the "game" of life is serious business, separating the winners from the losers allows us to sit back and laugh at ourselves, a vital human quality. If you always think like a winner, you will be a winner.

Idea: Become a winner. In every thought you have, every act you perform, everything you say, you have the choice of being optimistic or pessimistic, positive or negative. I can assure you that the optimists are always more successful at getting what they want than the pessimists. If you're an optimist, it indicates to those who can influence your promotion that you're prepared and confident. It also helps set you off from the rest of the pack.

Help: Live to Win (Harper & Row, 1989) by Victor Kiam shows you everything you need to know to win in business and achieve success. Victor Kiam was the man who bought Remington, the shaving company.

Become an Entrepreneur

In the old days, corporate types were completely different from entrepreneurial types. That was before we learned how to interbreed the two types into a hybrid. If you're not a hybrid, then you had better become one quickly if you want to get promoted. The corporate side tells you when it's best to follow policy and procedures to prove beyond any reasonable doubt that you're a loyal corporate soldier. Conversely, your entrepreneurial side will quickly remind you that although you are intensely loyal to the corporation, the corporation may not always be loyal to you.

Let's face it, you are not in Kansas anymore and the yellow brick road is full of potholes. Gone are the good old days when you could count on working for the same company for the rest of your life. Just ask any one of the 225,000 employees who used to work for IBM or the 200,000 AT&T employees who found themselves in the same boat in the turbulent 1980s and 90s. It's a fact that you'll change jobs during the course of your career, so accept it.

In many respects, you are really not working for a company at all, but rather yourself. Like any good entrepreneur, you are selling yourself, your talents, and what you know to a company that is willing to pay you what they think your credentials are worth. As you build on your credentials, start thinking like an entrepreneur. Here are several ideas that will help you get started:

1. Assess where you are now and identify the hurdles you must clear to get you where you want to go. Next, address how they're going to clear the hurdles.

2. List each of the promotional tenets on the back of your business card and make a commitment to do at least one thing each day to improve upon your expertise in one or more of the tenets.

3. Take a moment at the end of each day to write down what you will add to your action list in order to improve your credentials.

4. Remove the word "excuse" from your vocabulary. And phrases such as: "I don't have time," " I'm stuck," " I don't know what I want," and any others should no longer exist in your entrepreneurial frame of reference.

5. Start thinking like a entrepreneur. When they're playing golf, entrepreneurs only see the green. The corporate types only see sand traps.

Ultimately, you want to make yourself so valuable that the headhunters are tearing your door down to get at you and companies are having bidding wars to get your attention. As a corporate and entrepreneur hybrid, you'll develop the ability to see the big picture and know exactly what action to take to create the results you want. You'll know you are good because your peers will constantly look to you for direction and ideas. Your motivation will become unlimited so that when you run into obstacles, you'll treat them as challenges and exciting learning experiences rather than obstacles. Your self-confidence on the job will flow over to your personal life where everything is under control.

(?) **Help:** *The Vest Pocket Entrepreneur* (Prentice Hall, 1994) by David Rye is an excellent reference for anyone who wants to become an entrepreneur or sharpen their entrepreneurial skills.

Idea: Learn to visualize clearly how other high achievers think and act. Read and study what they have written. Listen to their tapes and go to seminars to hear them talk. Take a high achiever from work out to lunch and listen to everything they have to say. Learn everything you can from the masters.

Commit Yourself

Have you ever wondered why you never see mules racing in the Kentucky Derby? Mules are the plodders that you can rely on to always get you from Point A to Point B if they are given enough time, but they'll never win a horse race. That speedy task is reserved for thoroughbreds. Do you consider yourself a thoroughbred and do you believe that your commitment to the task will make you a winner? As you race to the finish line for that promotion you want, stop and take a moment to think about where you're going. Think about how you have your mind set on what you want to accomplish. Are there barriers in your way and do you see them in a positive perspective?

On his death bed, J. Paul Getty was asked, "Mr. Getty, you're one of the richest men in the world, but if you had your life to live over, what would you do differently?" He responded, "Oh, that's an easy question to answer. I'd go for bigger deals. I'd commit more!" I believe there's a direct correlation between the commitment you have to a cause, such as your promotion, and the achievement that you'll experience. The greater your commitment, the more motivation you will have. Both commitment and motivation feed off each other and must be in place before anything will happen. Don't be like the kamikaze pilot who flew more than 200 missions. He was committed, but he wasn't motivated enough to get the job done.

If you want to get committed to something, you need to clarify the objective of your commitment. What exactly do you want to achieve? Does it light a fire under you? Are you motivated? Has anyone ever told you, "Motivation is fine, but it doesn't last?" If motivation isn't backed with a commitment that you believe in, it won't last. The average human only uses about 20 percent of his or her brain power. We all have incredible reserve brain power and untapped resources to do whatever we commit ourselves to do.

Unfortunately, excuses are one of the biggest deterrents to commitment. We arm ourselves with all of the excuses we're capable of fabricating. How many times have you caught yourself saying, "Well, it's easy for other people to get fired up but not for me. I have a lot on my mind. Things aren't going the way I planned." There's an endless line of excuses that we have all used. Starting now, get rid of them!

In conclusion, commitment is an emotion that's an innate quality within each of us that excites us to accomplish something that's important. Once you've committed yourself to the task, you've got half the problem licked. Then, all you have to do to maintain your motivation over the long term is to actively pursue what you want to accomplish. If you do that consistently, the power of motivation will serve you well for the rest of your life.

● *Warning:* People's inability to get organized is responsible for a great majority of career failures. When you make a commitment to accomplish something, break it down into the tasks that you must complete to achieve success. Then, make a commitment to do them within a specific time frame.

Believe in Yourself

The starting point for both success and happiness is a healthy self-image. According to Dr. Joyce Brothers, a well-known psychologist, "An individual's self-image is the core of their personality. It affects every aspect of a person's human behavior including their ability to learn, their capacity to grow and change, their choice of friends, mates, and careers. It's no exaggeration to say that a strong positive self-image is the best possible preparation for success in life."

You must believe in yourself first if you want to achieve success and happiness. All of the self-induced motivational goal-setting and positive thinking steps you might go through won't work until after you have first accepted yourself. People with poor self-images often see how positive thinking works for others but never for them. Here are the primary causes of poor self-image and what you can do about them:

Negative society. Part of the problem stems from the fact that we live in a negative society that is constantly bombarding us with negative events. Scan any newspaper and it's a challenge to find anything positive on the front page. The typical comments that we all make reveal how prevalent negativity has become. Ask someone how they are doing and they'll tell you "Not too bad" or "Okay" rather than "Just great thank you." From now on, when someone asks how you're doing, say "Just great" even when you aren't feeling great. You'll feel better after you say it!

Reinforcement. Poor self-image can develop in a person when their ability, appearance, or intelligence has been ridiculed repeatedly by some authoritative person. This could be a parent, teacher, friends, or a boss. In many cases, the damage comes in the form of insinuations and innuendoes. How many times has an unintentional remark stirred you into blind fury? The net effect is that you'll begin to see yourself through the negative eyes of others. Don't let that happen to you.

Exaggeration. In some cases, an exaggerated statement can have a profound affect on one's self-image. You make a comment at a meeting and someone says, "That's just another one of your dumb ideas." What an exaggerated burden you have to carry. The implication of the comment is that all of your ideas are dumb, which of course is of course not true. Make sure you don't overreact to exaggerated comments.

Inferiority complex. A poor self-image could be due to an inferiority complex that was developed during childhood and carried over into adulthood. Once the poor self-image slide starts, the natural tendency is to feed off your inferiority feeling. Don't forget what's happened in the past, but don't dwell on it either!

Unfair comparisons. You can damage your self-image by making unfair comparisons of personal experiences. This happens when you compare your experience with the experience of another person and exaggerate their successes while downgrading your own successes. If you think that everything is always going perfect for everyone else but you, then you're living in a dream world.

Comparing features. We often trap ourselves into the dumb practice of comparing our worst features against someone else's best features. One woman consistently did that and as a result, became a scrubwoman on welfare. When she discovered her positive traits, like her ability to make people laugh, she started performing on Broadway and in Hollywood movies. Today, Phillis Diller is regarded as one of the top female comedians of all time.

When you combine all of the reasons people can come up with for having a poor self-image, there is little wonder why so many are crippled by this prevalent and contagious disease. To avoid getting the disease, it's important that you recognize the manifestations of poor self-image so that you can be more effective at dealing with your own self-image problems. When you can identify and face your self-image problems with confidence, the solution is on its way. So is your next promotion.

Idea: When you choose to develop a habit, you are also choosing the end result of that habit. Most habits are easy to acquire. Good habits are easy to live with and the bad ones are difficult to live with. Almost without exception, bad habits are acquired slowly over time and become a habit often before you know.

Apply the Power of Positive Thinking

In Norman Peale's book, *The Power of Positive Thinking,* he talked about the fact that most people think in terms of positive or negative mental attitudes. Although there are many facets of attitude, let's look at the positive side first. Positive attitude is in its finest form when you experience something that makes you feel good, particularly when you're feeling down. The power of positive thinking came to me when I was entering the compounds of IBM's Boulder, Colorado facility one morning and saw three blind men exiting a van in front of the main lobby. They were IBM employees who had come to work just as I had with the obvious exception that they needed a ride.

My mind quickly diverted to the major confrontation meeting I had scheduled with my boss in 15 minutes to discuss problems we were encountering with a major account. The noise from the van caught my attention again as the blind men exited the van, laughing as they helped each other out. Fascinated, I followed them into the lobby and down the hall as they continued to help each other find their way to their respective work areas with smiles on their faces and laughter in their hearts. At the end of the episode, I concluded that I had nothing to be negative about, and to be honest with you, I was ashamed of myself after witnessing the positive attitudes that these men had just displayed. I was the one with the handicap!

If you ever think you're down and out, make sure you put things in their proper perspective. It's one of the quickest ways I know of to get the power of positive thinking back into your brain.

The subsequent confrontation meeting with my boss turned out to be one of the most constructive meetings I've ever had thanks to the three blind men. I started the meeting by saying, "Yeah boss, we have a few problems but here's what I think we can do to solve them." Icebergs melted away during the remainder of the meeting and every problem I thought we had got resolved.

Be Determined in Everything You Do

Some people are superstars when it comes to using their determination to recovering from major problems and setbacks. Atlantic Richfield's CEO, Lod Cook, is a classic example of one who used determination to conquer every problem he confronted. Lod grew up during The Depression in a small Louisiana town called Grand Cane. His home was heated by a wood fireplace, featured an outhouse round back, and a well for water in the front. Despite his meager surroundings, his parents always encouraged him to embrace his determination to get ahead.

Lod joined the Atlantic Richfield Company shortly after he graduated from college as a clerk in the personnel department. He enjoyed working with people and over time, discovered how to get a wide range of people to pull toward a common goal. In 1977, Lod became president of Arco's transportation division and represented Arco's interest in the Trans-Alaska Pipeline System. The pipeline was owned by seven major corporations who all had to collaborate on the construction of the line with state and federal government officials. Disaster hit when one of the major pumping stations burned down.

Most of the people working on the project had extensive pipeline experience, which Lod didn't have. In searching for a way to solve the limited pumping capabilities, Lod suggested using an untested compound called DRA (drag-reducing agent). His thought was to blend DRA with crude oil to reduce the drag so that more oil could be pumped through the remaining stations. Lod's associates all laughed at the idea. In his determination, Lod mixed DRA with oil in a lab and discovered that it worked.

The testing was the easy part of solving the problem. The hard part was convincing the other six competing corporations and owners of the pipeline to try an idea their experts had previously dismissed as stupid. Lod pulled the team together and convinced them to agree to try DRA. The original pipeline was designed to carry 1.4 million barrels of oil a day. DRA increased the capacity to more than 4 million barrels a day. Lod's determination paid off and he was later promoted to CEO proving once again that determination pays off in the promotional game.

Idea: Be good at what you do and expand upon your innate ability to do more. Become a master at what you do now. Know everything there is to know about your company's products and services, the industry you're in, and the makeup of your major competitors. Go to training programs and read all of the applicable trade journals. And look like a professional. Upgrade your wardrobe and appearance so people will notice who you are. As more and more of them start coming to you for advice and consultations, those who are responsible for promoting you will take notice.

Wait for Your Best Shot

You'll never win a game all at once. Basketball is a perfect example. It's an event that's filled with 48-minute streams of possessions, blocks, shots, steals, and passes, just as a year in your business life is made up of a 365-day stream of events. It isn't humanly possible for a basketball team to score on every possession just as it's not possible for you to win every encounter you run into at work. No matter what your role is at work, there are always smaller encounters that fit within a larger whole like skirmishes within a battle, battles within a campaign, and campaigns within a war. Each small victory improves the odds that you will ultimately triumph. Wait for your best shot.

Magic Johnson was a classic example of a man who waited for his best shot. If you ever saw this man play basketball, it was like watching poetry in motion. During the course of a game, the ball got inbound to him. He knew exactly what he had to do to orchestrate his game. He'd start off by waving his teammates to certain areas of the court as he'd dribbled out to the wing, backing his defender up. You saw his eyes simultaneously watching all the players, checking the game and shot clock so that he knew precisely when to make his move.

Somewhere in the tempo of the play, an alarm went off in Johnson's inner ear that told him it's time to take his shot. He switched the dribble to his left hand, lifted his right shoulder, and turned his head toward the baseline like he was getting ready to shoot. His defenders reacted by shifting their weight toward the baseline, just as Johnson lowered his other shoulder and spun around in the opposite direction as he sliced into the lane drawing two more defenders. As they converged to block his path, Johnson began to make a hook shot, which caused his defenders to leap into the air forming a 10-foot human fence with outstretched arms. Johnson proceeded to bring the ball through the predictable arc of a hook shot, then suddenly changed the angle of the ball with his wrist, and snapped a pass to a Laker teammate who was coming in from the opposite baseline. Nobody touched him as he jammed the ball through the hoop, making the shot.

The trademark of winners is their gold-plated precision inner clock that they rely on to tell them when to make the right move and the right shot. They'll also have an aerial view of everything that's going on in the game. Treat your efforts to get yourself promoted like you would if you were playing in a professional basketball game. Like every game, there comes a moment that defines winning from losing. A true winner understands and seizes that moment by giving an effort that's so intense, nobody can stop them from succeeding.

Idea: If you want to get noticed, make yourself the happiest person in the place. One of the best ways to cheer yourself up is to cheer everybody else up. A wise man once said, "He who stops being better stops being any good. Impossible is a word to be found only in the dictionary of losers."

Motivate People to Listen

Getting people to listen to your ideas can be challenging. First, they have to concentrate on what you're saying as they fight off their thoughts and feelings that are also competing for their attention. Next, they have to relate how your idea fits into their own experience in order to develop the proper mental picture. On top of all that, they have to be patient and wait for you to build your idea one word at a time. Listeners are also concerned that your idea may require a comment from them to get it implemented.

When you've asked someone to listen to your idea, make sure in advance that you have something to say that's worth listening to. Are your thoughts interesting and easy to grasp? Do you make your main points up front so that the person you're talking to can think, "Hey, this may be a good idea that's worth listening to"? If you drag it out, you risk irritating your listeners and subsequently turning their thoughts off.

Your first challenge is to sell your listeners on listening. Tell them up front about your idea and what they're going to gain by listening. The bottom line should be the most intriguing part of your whole idea, which summarizes your idea in one or two sentences with emphasis placed on the benefits and features of the idea. Start with it first because the first two minutes of your presentation are critical if you want to get them to listen. That's when listeners will decide to listen further to what you have to say or stop listening because they're no longer interested in your idea. Here's an example of a bottom-line statement:

> "Jim, I have an idea that I would like to discuss with you. If we consolidate our two respective departments, we'll save the company in excess of a million dollars a year and we'll both get the promotions that we want."

In the example, I used the possibility of a promotion to motivate Jim to listen to what I had to say about the consolidation idea. Although he may be skeptical about the implied promotion (that is, who's going to be the new boss of the consolidated groups), he'll listen to what you have to say to at least satisfy his curiosity. Your next challenge is to link Jim's thinking with yours. Somewhere in the conversation, you want Jim to take over part ownership of your idea. Once he does that, you've sold him. Instead of asking him, "What do you think of MY idea?" ask, "What do you think about working with me to consolidate OUR respective departments?" to establish joint ownership in the idea.

Another way to link your listener's thinking with yours is to compare his understanding with what you have already said. For example, you might say, "Jim, based on your statement, do you agree that we both should present the consolidation idea to the executive committee?" If the other person isn't giving you any feedback, you'll have changed your question into a two-directional question: "Jim, would you be willing to make a joint presentation with me to the executive committee?" Here are several other tips that will help get people to listen to your ideas:

Control your risks. Whenever you propose an idea to someone, you put them in a bind. There's a chance they will lose something if they accept your idea. If they don't buy into it, they risk losing what they might have gained. Once you've told them about your idea, they can't go back to the way things were before. They have to accept the responsibility for making a decision that can have positive or negative consequences. People generally exaggerate the risk when making decisions. To get people to view the risk realistically, remind them of the risk of *not* implementing your idea.

Get their attention. One of the biggest mistakes we often make when we present our ideas is that we think people are listening as long as they're sitting quietly. We keep talking because there is so much we want to say, and we can't resist what seems like a good chance to get it all in. And we do not want our thought patterns interrupted by remarks or questions. When a person interrupts us, he's telling us that he has to stop listening for a moment to get clarification on an issue. If you respond with, "Why don't you wait until I'm done," you risk shutting down all of the person's listening mechanisms. If you don't feel an immediate response is appropriate, you might say, "I'll cover your question in just a moment. If I don't, please interrupt me." Now your listener will continue to follow your presentation to see if his question gets answered.

Make it attractive. No matter what the idea or topic is, you have the power to make it dull or stimulating, depressing or inspiring. Even if the other person is dragging you down, come back and give the discussion a lift by displaying a burst of enthusiasm. If you can make the topic exciting to your listener, you'll sell him on your idea.

Make it easy. To sell your idea, you have to satisfy the needs of the other person. That's relatively easy if you keep a couple of major points in mind: Express your idea in the first part of the conversation and immediately check with your listener to see if she understands and agrees with your sales points. Be patient if she makes objections and answer all of her questions. In fact, encourage her to ask questions. If they're not asking any questions, they may not be listening to your pitch. If they make a point that you agree with, tell them you agree with what they said. If they make a point that you disagree with, ask probing questions to make sure you understand exactly what's bothering them before you recommend a solution.

People often give way to their desire to explain their idea all at once rather than presenting it in a slower, controlled pace. They're afraid of getting a "no" response, which they believe they can change once their listener sees the whole picture. In the process, they defeat themselves by flooding the other person with more information than they can handle. If they determine that it's too much work to sift out what you're saying and keep track of what doesn't make sense, they will stop listening.

(?) *Help:* Michael Landon was one of Hollywood's greatest motivators on and off the set. For three decades, Michael used love to motivate people to listen to him. The powerful word of "love" is seldom used in the psychological analysis of what it takes to be motivated, but it is at the heart of establishing true listening as Michael proved. Michael treated everyone who worked for or with him as if they were just as important as he was. Within his network of people, he always gave more than he received. The members of Michael's network could call on him as their mentor, silent partner, and true friend. He treated everybody in his network as valued members of his family and openly honored their contributions to his show *Highway to Heaven*. As a result, whenever he talked to someone, they always listened to what he had to say.

Idea: Apply some moderation in everything you do. We are often tempted to rush into implementing our new ideas at the expense of the other things that we should be doing. Use moderation as the mechanism to remind yourself that great accomplishments are made and objectives are reached when well-thought-out programs of activities are pursued comfortably day by day.

Conquer Your Fears

Even the *sound* of the word "fear" brings chills to one's spine. Fear is one of the biggest inhibitors that can short-circuit your motivation and your attempts to get yourself promoted. Debilitating fear is highly contagious and can be passed on from generation to generation. If your parents constantly warned you about the evil of failing when you were a child, you probably carry some bad fear cells in the back of your brain. It's time to get them out of there because they will inhibit your promotion. To do this, you need to understand how fear drives failure.

According to Webster's, fear is an emotion that can be very healthy, helpful, and even lifesaving. When we were young, fear taught us not to touch a hot stove a second time or to not jump off something that was too high. Conversely, fear can be very destructive, emotionally paralyzing, and even deadly. It's interesting to note that the definition starts out with the good attributes of fear. We all know this from our past experiences.

As we got older, we started to develop a healthy fear of authority. If we broke a speeding law, we had to pay a fine, which we didn't like doing so the fear of another fine kept us within the speed limit most of the time. The fear of getting an F in class prevented us from telling our instructor what we really thought about him. Over time, we learned to respect and not ignore the good side of fear.

The bad side of fear causes you to focus on things that you should not fear like whether or not you're going to get promoted. It carries with it devastating baggage of failure that can cause serious emotional problems. "If I don't get that position, will people think I'm a failure?" For some people, fear can cause serious medical problems such as high blood pressure and even death from a heart attack. Fortunately for most of us, fear is subtler but no less damning. It can literally stop you from doing things that you should be doing, which propagates your failure. For example, your fear of not getting promoted may stop you from pursuing any promotional activities thereby relegating you to the same old job for the rest of your life. That's the position the janitor in our building took when he told me, "I'm as low as I can go, and that's the way I like it." I guess there is nothing wrong with that except that this guy has a BS in computer science and a giant fear of failure.

A more dramatic example of how bad fear can cause debilitating behavior occurred at Lake Tahoe recently. A friend of mine was playing in a social tennis tournament that was sponsored by the resort where he was staying. The tournament had just started and he was playing against an older, in supposed good shape gentleman, who raised his racket to serve the first ball and suddenly fell over from an apparent heart attack. Everybody was rushing around to see what they could do while they waited for the ambulance to arrive.

By the time the ambulance finally got this fellow to the hospital, he was pronounced dead on arrival. My friend rode with him to the hospital and after the announcement, the emergency room physician asked, "Why didn't you administer CPR on the court? It probably would have saved his life." My friend's response was, "I was afraid I would break his ribs." The doctor ended the conversation by saying, "My God, man, anybody can survive with a few broken ribs." It took my friend several years to overcome the fact that he had allowed his fear to prevent him from possibly saving someone's life.

Your first step at conquering failure is to learn to recognize the difference between good and bad fear. Good fear allows you to protect and preserve that which is good for you, your team, and your organization. Good fear usually focuses on the long-term consequences of doing what is right. Bad fear prevents you from doing what is good and right for yourself and others. It typically focuses on the short-term consequences of not doing something.

How do you detect when bad fear is diverting you from what you want to accomplish and what can you do about it? The answer to the question is you have to be extremely honest with yourself. This can become a more difficult exercise for men than women. If you're one of those macho guys who have been taught to fear nothing, then you have been taught to lie to yourself. The only human being who can not feel fear is one that is brain dead. What do you want to accomplish and what fears do you have if you fail to accomplish whatever it is you want? Write them down.

Your next step is to review in detail every fear you have written down and ask yourself, "Is there anything I can do to control or eliminate this fear?" If your answer is yes, set up an action plan to make the fear go away. If your answer is no then forget it. For example, let's say that one of your fears about getting promoted is that you don't know how to communicate well in meetings, which will be a key responsibility in your new position. Can you do something about it? You answer yes when you decide to join Toastmasters to improve your presentation skills. Your second fear had to do with what people would think if you don't get promoted to the position that everybody knows you want. Because you can't control what other people will think about an event that has not yet occurred, the fear is unfounded and therefore irrelevant. Get it out of your head so that you can pursue bigger and better things. If you can conquer fear, then your task at conquering failure is relatively easy.

Any failure that you experience can be a great teacher and even a powerful mentor to your future if you accept it with the right attitude. My uncle once told me, "Dave, a man who never fails is one who never makes a decision." Assuming that you plan to continue to make decisions throughout your career, then you have to accept the fact that you will make some bad decisions. If you make a conscious effort to assign any of your past and future failures to the role of being your teachers, then failure will reinforce everything you do.

(?) *Help:* *Starting From "NO"* (Upstart Publishing, 1999) by Azriela Jaffe covers 10 strategies you can use to overcome your fear of rejection in any business situation.

Idea: Trust is the lubrication that makes it possible for organizations to work. It's also a critical component of motivation.

Chapter 5

Communicating With Power and Influence

The power of the sword is mightier than the pen, at least in the story that I am about to tell you. Several years ago, I worked for a subsidiary of Phillip Morris. At the time, I was a director of all the departments that nobody else wanted including procurement, warehousing, distribution, customer service, production, and MIS. On one fine Monday morning, the senior vice president from corporate headquarters flew in to our remote location in Ventura, California and announced that he wanted us to install a computerized manufacturer resource planning (MRP) system. At the time, MRP was the highly touted and popular business buzzword whose flames were fanned by the system's creator, Olie White. Olie conducted a highly successful national seminar program that propagated the benefits of MRP, which was designed to capture all of the related costs associated with the manufacturing of products. That in a nutshell is what MRP is all about, although you can buy a multitude of books that will refine the definition down to whatever level of detail you can tolerate. Because the system was to be computerized, and the MIS department reported to me, the charter to implement MRP was assigned to me.

The challenge one faces when implementing MRP is communicating system requirements effectively to all groups and departments in the organization that are affected by MRP. For example, because MRP identifies the absolute cost of products, the sales and marketing organizations are vitally concerned about product pricing and want to be involved in defining pricing parameters. The accounting and finance people are concerned about the integrity of the numbers you're using, and administration wants to know how you determine overhead. Unfortunately, these department did not report to me and they all had something to say about what should be included or not included in the new system. To solve the dilemma, an inter-department team was formed to resolve a myriad of outstanding cost and pricing issues. Three month later, the team was no closer to resolving basic system definitions than they were when they started, and the squabbling continued.

Somehow, the senior vice president heard about our dilemma and scheduled a meeting with the MRP project team to discuss the status of the project. One bright Monday morning, we all showed up for the meeting to hear what our vice president had to say about our efforts. I will never forget his opening remarks: "MRP team members, it has been brought to my attention that you are encountering some difficulty on agreeing on how to implement my MRP system. Let me provide you with some guidance that will help you focus on the task at hand. If my MRP system is not fully implemented within the next three months, you will all be fired with no exceptions. Are there any questions?"

There were no questions and as everyone quietly left the meeting room, we all had a solid appreciation of what this man had just verbally communicated to each of us. Our vice president had demonstrated how to communicate with power and influence.

The inter-department squabbling instantly stopped and the MRP system was successfully implemented within that allotted three months. The power of communication, if properly exploited, will serve you well as you climb up the organizational ladder.

● *Warning:* Although the pen may be mightier than the sword, neither is mightier than the mouth, especially when it come to creating first impressions with people who count in social settings. Voice communication is second only to body language as a means of communicating in social settings. In face-to-face interactions, it isn't enough to be physically attractive. The moment you open your mouth, you either confirm or deny an initial impression a person has about you. Abe Lincoln once said, "It's better to keep your mouth shut and let others think you're a fool than to open it and confirm that you are in fact a fool." If you sound harsh and abrasive, you probably will be viewed as harsh and abrasive. If you sound timid and insecure, you will be considered as such. And if you sound strong and confident, chances are you'll be thought of that way.

(?) *Help:* *Powerful Communication Skills* (Career Press, 1998) by Colleen McKenna is written in a friendly, easy-to-follow format that's filled with easy-to-implement communication tips you can immediately start using immediately.

What Effective Communications Can Do For You

A large percentage of business communication is spoken in either face-to-face confrontations or on the telephone. The way you speak and say things can help you direct the behavior of others and promote your growth and development. Face-to-face speaking is probably the most effective means of praising, reprimanding, encouraging, or otherwise reacting to other people. It can also help you get along better with others, something that's necessary for the performance of your job. For example, setting mutual goals and agreeing on a work plan to accomplish them requires the use of effective speaking and listening skills. It can also work in the reverse. If you're in an office or other work setting where two or more people are not on good speaking terms, there is invariably a slowdown in the workflow. If you're one of the non-communicators, and it gets noticed by anyone who can influence your promotion, you'll lose points regardless of whose fault it is.

Regardless of what we do for a living, we are all in the communication business. How often we manage to say the right things directly affects not only the opportunities that come our way, but also the level of personal satisfaction we enjoy. In a recent *Harvard Business Review* poll, a majority of the executives surveyed named communication skills as a major factor in determining who was or was not qualified for upper management positions within their organizations. Although most of us are aware of the importance of communications, we rarely give communication skills the attention they deserve. Instead, we go through life wrestling with seemingly unrelated issues, such as, personal and work relationships without stopping to consider how well we are verbally expressing ourselves. Are you saying the right things?

Saying the right thing is based on one critical, but often overlooked element in the verbal communications process: the clarity factor. The clarity factor is a subtle, but essential element that makes verbal communication productive and rewarding. It means that when we speak, we are also understood. When that consistently happens, verbal communication becomes a comfortable and rewarding process. Common frustrations from being misunderstood are avoided and our stress is reduced. Your interaction in both your personal and professional life takes on a new and exciting sense of human connection when there's clarity in your speech.

Speaking can also help you learn about yourself and what's going on around you. In any discussion involving negotiations or problem solving, you learn by talking and listening. If you're negotiating, the most important thing for you to learn is the person's bottom line, the point at which a settlement can be reached. If you're in a problem solving discussion with several participants, each might have part of a solution. It's only by talking to them that the parts can be pulled together to form a whole solution. If you're consistently successful at doing that, you will have mastered an essential communication skill that will serve you well as you ascend the corporate ladder.

? *Help:* Sue Gaulke's *101 Ways to Captivate a Business Audience* (AMACOM, 1996) show you all kinds of great ways to grab the attention of your audience so that they'll remember every word you say at your next presentation.

Who's Listening?

Some people operate like one-way radios. They are fully capable of transmitting words out at extremely rapid rates but because they have damaged receivers, they are incapable of listening to what anybody else says. Your need to listen increases exponentially as you move up the organizational ladder. You're going to be bombarded by everybody who thinks they have an idea and it will be your responsibility to listen to what they have to say so you can make informed decisions about which ideas are worth pursuing. Following are four steps you can take that will help you become a better listener.

1. Eliminate filters. We all have them. Filters are the smoke-screens we listen through when someone talks to us. Your filters are designed to stop you from receiving words when they convince you that you're wasting your time listening to someone. They'll also stop you from listening if you're not interested in what someone is saying. Control your filters and make a concerted effort to listen to everyone, even if you intuitively know they have nothing to say.

2. Control your mouth. Think twice before you speak when you are supposed to be listening. Most people will spend time thinking about what they want to say when someone is talking to them, so they can't possibly be listening. An astute listener will wait until a person is through talking and say, "Let me think about what you just said before I comment." Then they think before they speak, with the full benefit of having heard everything the other person had to say.

3. Listen with purpose. You are listening to achieve something that is good for you, which should make the process a lot easier to accommodate. You're listening to be amiable, to allow someone to vent their frustrations because they trust you, to get feedback on a question you have asked, or for a variety of other reasons. Once you recognize that you have a personal stake in the listening game, your listening abilities will become more focused.

4. Check for accuracy. If you're listening to some heavy dialog that perhaps involves a major problem, your antenna should already be extended to hear everything the person is saying. Are you properly interpreting their words? One way to find out is to break your code of silence when listening and ask appropriate questions: "Let me make sure I understand what you just said..." or "Are you telling me that...."

Listening is time well spent in developing any relationship. In fact, you cannot have a meaningful relationship with anybody when you are not willing to listen. As you practice your listening skills, you will sharpen your intuition. You'll also start to see similarities in people, which will make you more sensitive to their needs and a better judge of character. All of these attributes will serve you well in your promotional campaign.

(?) *Help: The Lost Art of Listening* (Guilford Press, 1996) by Michael Nichols is a comprehensive guide that addresses why people don't listen and what you can do to get them to listen to what you have to say.

Know How to Use the Telephone

The telephone is key to all phases of communications from introducing a new idea and testing the waters on something you want to do, to getting feedback. In today's volatile business environment, the telephone is often the only effective way to address constant change in a timely manner because many of the people you need to contact are difficult to see face-to-face. The use of a telephone as a contact tool can be significantly more efficient than making a personal contact. Of course, there will always be situations that demand face-to-face contact, but even these situation often require the use of a telephone to initiate a meeting time.

The main difference between telephone and face-to-face communications is obvious. When you're on the telephone, the person you're talking to is not physically present. There is no face-to-face contact, no eye contact, and no physical presence to give you clues as to how well you're communicating. It's this potential for depersonalization that creates the bulk of the issues you must address when you communicate by phone. Your voice, your choice of words, your ability to build rapport, and to listen effectively are all critical in phone communications. Following are several communication techniques that work great on the telephone.

Create presence. Presence is the level of comfort and confidence you project when you're on the telephone. Winston Churchill personified presence when he spoke on the radio when England was being ripped by German air raids during World War II. The English people felt that he was speaking to them personally, a trait that you must learn to master every time you use the telephone. Voice presence is created by tone, pace, diction, inflection, confidence, and your level of enthusiasm. You also have to be quick on your feet to recognize, sight unseen, what the other person is saying so that you can quickly develop an appropriate response. A 31-year-old friend of mine called a high-tech silicon valley firm for an interview with their 60-year-old CEO who told him, "You sound young." My friend responded with confidence and enthusiasm: "If you think I *sound* young, wait until you see what I look like." Needless to say, the CEO couldn't wait and the interview was set. Although the display of enthusiasm may come naturally in face-to-face meetings, it requires a special effort on the telephone.

Sound interested. The more modulated you make your voice, the more interesting you sound when you emphasize words. For example, "I think the time to do it is NOW" emphasizes the importance of timing in a phone call. Make sure you balance your assertiveness with respect for whomever you're talking to by not sounding impatient, annoyed, judgmental, arrogant, or condescending.

Build rapport. If you can't relate to the person you're talking to on the telephone, you'll not be able to sell them on any idea you might have, and they will only hear about half of what you have to say. This is as much a characteristic of human nature as it is a rule to telecommunications. Although rapport is often associated with an opening question like, "How was your weekend?" it should flow throughout the call. If you don't know the person you're talking to, rapport may initially be difficult to establish until after you have made several calls and gained their confidence. The time to build rapport on a first call is often at the end of the call, when you ask, "So are you planning to get away for the holiday weekend?"

Share information. Knowing when and how to share information about yourself is also part of building rapport. Sharing personal information can open the door for the other person to share personal information with you. In most businesses, important transactions don't occur unless a relationship has been established. Your promotion will be partially dependent upon sub-relationships you establish over the telephone.

Query for information. Knowing how to ask the right question to solicit needed information is at the heart of successful telecommunicating. The answers you receive from your questions allow you to better position whatever it is you're trying to accomplish with the phone call. Unfortunately, it's easy to fall into the telephone trap of talking and asking questions first because you're anxious to get the conversation started. Avoid the impulse of showing them your cards until you know what their hand looks like. For example, if you're calling your boss to see if she will give you permission to attend the COMDEX computer show in Las Vegas, your opening question might be: "What do you think about COMDEX?" If she tells you she thinks it's a waste of time, you might not want to ask to go when there is a high probability that you'll be turned down. In this instance, your question stirred up an objection, which is not necessarily bad. At least you know where you stand and have to opportunity to probe with additional questions to find out why she thinks it is a waste of time.

Listen for clues. Telephone communication experts will tell you that most of the information that is communicated in face-to-face encounters comes from nonverbal signals, such as body language. This presents some obvious problems in telecommunications where you can't see nonverbal signals. You can however pick up on non-verbal clues by listening carefully to a person's tone of voice, emphasis, pace, and diction. Although the ability to listen is important to face-to-face communications, it is critical to telecommunications. To gain as much as you possibly can from a telephone conversation, listen not only to what someone says, but how they say it—or do not say it. Does the tone of their voice sound interested or uninterested? Is the pace of their conversation relaxed or anxious? For example, if their voice trails off at the end of a sentence or is soft on key words, they may be giving you a clue about their lack of commitment or interest in the theme of your conversation. Also, listen to the kinds of questions you are asked; this will give you clues about their level of interest.

Position the conversation. Most people are more than willing to answer properly presented questions if you tell them that you value their opinion before you ask the questions. If you properly position your question, you'll get flooded with all of the information you need. If you have asked the right questions, listened to what the other person has to say, and you took notes, you should have everything you need to position your call objective so that it incorporates the views of the person you're talking to. By knowing their perceptions, preferences, and needs, you will be able to customize what you say to get exactly what you want.

Check for status. Checking is a way to get feedback from the person to see if you are both on the same page. You check by asking questions to gauge a person's reaction to what you're saying like, "Do you agree with my position?" Because you can't see the reaction of the other person, checking with questions is essential to the telecommunication process. It helps avoid waiting until the end of a call to find out if a person is interested in your idea or understands what you're talking about. For example, suppose you have just called your boss to find out what he thought about the presentation you made at yesterday's executive staff meeting.

You're particularly interested in knowing if he appreciated the significance of the projected sales numbers you presented. After you briefly explain how you arrived at the numbers, you might ask a simple question: "Did my numbers make sense and do you have any recommendations that would improve that part of my presentation?" Although you ultimately want to know what he thought about your overall presentation, you can't check on that issue until you know if he understood the quantitative part of it.

As you perfect the different telephone techniques that I've covered, take notes when you are on the telephone. Notes not only help you focus on important things the person says, they help you position your strategy base on important words the person says. Salespeople are keenly aware of the importance of telephone note-taking. An outstanding saleswoman I know (Kathy) closed a million-dollar deal when her customer was discussing a competitor's lower price and said, "On the surface, it looks like a good deal." Clearly, the customer wasn't sure that Kathy had a good deal. When Kathy reminded the customer that he had always received high-quality computers and service from her company, the customer agreed that it was not worth switching to an unknown competitor.

(?) *Help: Phone Tactics for Instant Influence* (Dembner Books, 1990) by John Truitt is one of the best books out that teaches you everything you'll need to know to influence anyone when you are on the telephone.

Keep Your Arrogance to Yourself

From the moment you start talking to anybody on the telephone or face-to-face, it's important that you project confidence without sounding arrogant or pushy. The real problem with arrogance, apart from the fact that it turns people off, is that complacency and a lack of imagination usually accompany it. If you exude this image in your conversation to anybody—from the lowest to the highest level—you will severely cripple your chances of getting promoted. Here's a story that illustrates my point.

Karen was the controller of a Fortune 500 company and was incredibly sharp at understanding and managing any company's finances. Backed with a master's degree in computer science and a CPA degree, Karen was considered a "shoe in" for the chief financial officer position that was vacated when "good ol' Ed" retired. However, Karen had a habit of communicating with all of the arrogance of a cobra while on the telephone to subordinates and peers.

Just before her promotion was about to be announced, the company's CEO decided to take "a walkabout" through the accounting department to find out what Karen's people thought about her. When he discovered that her colleagues thought she was one of the most arrogant people they had ever known, her promotion was canceled. Karen resigned from the company the next day. Never underestimate the importance of anyone you talk to. Although they may not have a direct say in whether you'll be promoted, they can torpedo your chances with a single statement! Here's how to control your conversations:

Open the door with a hinge. A hinge is an effective way to connect to someone you don't know. For example, you can use a referral hinge to open a conversation: "I am calling at the suggestion of a mutual friend of ours," or you can use the research hinge by saying, "I read your great article in the company newsletter and...."

Open with why. You need to tell people you don't know why you want to talk to them in a well-coordinated opening statement. If it's a formal or semi-formal conversation, briefly state your objective and the purpose of the call. Your purpose is the flip side of your objective and tells the person you're talking to what's in it for them. If you anticipate that it will be a long call, you may want to set an agenda so that the two of you are in agreement as to what needs to be discussed. Your opening statement might go something like this: "Joe, thank you for taking the time to talk with me to discuss volunteers for your special projects team. I would like to head up the team (your objective). My purpose for calling you is to present my qualifications that will assure the team's success."

Create a bridge. Once you have successfully opened a conversation, you may think you're ready to start talking. Even if the conversation is going extremely well, bite your lip to keep yourself from talking first, and listen to whatever the other person says first before you present any of your ideas. Get as much information as you can from them so that you can tailor your ideas with words that will have a maximum positive effect. For example, you might follow up on your opening statement with a question: "Joe, did you get a chance to review my qualifications for the team leader position that I e-mailed to you yesterday? What did you think?"

Control objections. Objections can come at any point during a conversation, regardless of how effective your opening statement was or how well you established a bridge in the conversation. Objections are a vital part of the human communications process, so don't despair when someone throws a verbal dart at you. Look at the positive side: It's a solid indication that they understand exactly what you want. If you can't deal with objections, you will substantially handicap your communications effectiveness. Make sure you understand exactly what the person's objections are before you counter their objections with a response. You can do this by asking an appropriate question like, "Joe, you said that you don't believe that I am qualified for the team lead position. Could you be more specific?"

Turn off with style. On occasion, you may find yourself engaged in a conversation with a person who has nothing to say that interests you. How do you turn them off without offending them? Wait for them to take a breath, and then jump in with a reason to end the conversation. Ask them what time is it and then say, "I'm late for a meeting. Can we continue this very interesting conversation at another time?" You'll get an automatic "yes" answer and you've ended the conversation without offending the person.

Avoid using slang, informal, or casual speech in any of your business-related conversations unless it is with a dear and trusted friend. With rare exception, telling jokes will never win you any points; they could actually cost you points if you offend someone. I don't care how clever you think you are, leave your clever remarks out of your conversation. Make every conversation clear, articulate your points, and talk in a friendly, professional tone that's genuine.

(?) Help: *Winning Telephone Tips* (Career Press, 1997) by Paul Timm covers 30 fast and profitable tips for making the best use of your phone time. You'll also learn about innovative ways to prevent someone from wandering off the topic.

Idea: Always say no with style. Any fool can just say no and walk away from the situation. The person who can say no and offer an explanation has style. They're true professionals and the ones who get promoted.

Communicate Through Your Heart

Have you ever talked to someone who was looking you straight in the eye, and when you were done, they didn't hear a word you said? You knew they were not listening because their eyelids were struggling to stay open or they had a dazed look on their face. I've had this happen to me and wondered why they weren't listening when I finally figured out that it was my fault. Although everybody knows that you hear with your ears and see with your eyes, I had only been talking to their ears. Their eyes decided that they had nothing to do with the conversation and they subsequently closed. If you want to achieve excellence in communications, you had better learn the technique of not only speaking to the ear of your listener, but going for their eyes as well. Why the eyes? Because the eyes are the key to opening one's heart.

If you communicate first to the ear with a point, and then to the heart with an illustration, watch your listener's eyes light up. You'll know that you have helped them see with their heart what they have just heard with their ears. Their lips will curl up as they smile in recognition, as you rush back to their ears again to register another communication point. This is the art of successful communication that you must use to keep yourself in a promotable position.

If you don't learn how to communicate to a person's ears, eyes, and heart, you'll find yourself out in left field. One great way to communicate to someone's heart is by using humor because everybody loves to laugh, and humor paves the way to heartfelt communication. Hearing the truth can be boring, but hearing it presented with humor can produce warmth of recognition from the heart. The classic way to introduce bad news is by asking the question, "Do you want me to tell you the good news first or the bad news first?" The presentation of the bad news will definitely capture the listener's ear. The prospect of the good news will potentially capture their heart.

I once sat in a board of directors' meeting when the chairman announced the bad news: "The bad news is we've been taken over by XYZ Corporation." Needless to say, everybody in the boardroom heard what the chairman had just said with their ears. When he said, "The good news is the acquisition offer includes a 25-percent increase in our current stock price," he had captured the hearts of all the stockholders. If you can get people to think with you and get them personally involved in what you're saying, you will be well on your way to becoming an excellent communicator.

● *Warning:* Loose lips sink ships—and careers. Be very careful about communicating highly confidential information that could damage your career if it became known to the wrong person(s) that you were the source of the leak.

(?) *Help: How to Make Winning Presentations* (Career Press, 1997) by Paul Timm includes 30 action tips for getting your ideas across with clarity and impact.

Hold Dynamic Meetings

Like the weather, everybody complains about meetings, but few know what to do about them. Despite the fact that meetings, unlike the weather, are a human creation, we often have no more control over a meeting than we do the weather. However, we live in a time when we believe that two or more heads are better than one when key decisions need to be made in a meeting.

One scene in the movie *Wall Street* crystallized for me the biggest reason why meetings break down. A large corporate meeting with hundreds of people in attendance was taking place and company executives were arguing with impatient shareholders as to why profits were down. In a sensible world, these forces should have been working together to solve their mutual problem. Instead, each special-interest group wanted results that would benefit them. One of the corporate execs, played by Michael Douglas, grabbed the microphone and abruptly took over the meeting when he shouted, "Greed is good." That single phrase captured the way all of the diverse groups in the room were thinking. They instantly jelled into a single force behind their newfound "greed is good" leader.

The balance of the meeting focused on alternative ways the corporation could maximize profits. The initial problem that was encountered in the fictional *Wall Street* meeting was the fact that there was no central theme established before the meeting started. It took a disproportionate amount of meeting time to arrive at a theme that everyone could agree upon. Your success at conducting effective meetings—where participants can focus on the central theme and objective of the meeting will play an important role at winning you promotional points.

Much of people's impatience with meetings stems from the time it takes to produce real value. No wonder nobody wants to attend a meeting. How often do we ask meeting participants to bring prepared thoughts into the meeting? Do we tell attendees what the exact purpose of the meeting is beforehand? Not usually, and the result is that most meetings take twice as long as they should because nobody was given an opportunity to prepare. You're lucky if anything gets accomplished. Give serious thought to meetings you're responsible for or to the ones you're asked to attend. Get hard-nosed about what you want to accomplish at every meeting you sponsor.

(?) *Help: Secrets of Power Presentations, Second Edition* by Micki Holliday (Career Press, 2000) shows you how to overcome your fear of public speaking so you can become a "star" presenter at your next meeting.

A Checklist for Your Next Meeting

Many people have little conception of what it takes to set up a meeting and make it function effectively. Smooth and efficient problem-solving meetings don't just happen. They evolve over time and if they are properly organized and planned, they can do wonders to your promotional prospects. Conversely, if you're the one who is responsible for a bad meeting, you could lose more promotion points than you will care to think about.

Meetings should never be held to solve problems that are too unimportant for the level of the group or that are outside the group's area of authority. However, if the group has been chartered by senior management to resolve a problem that's outside of their authority, then it's appropriate for them to address higher-level problems. Following are eight procedural and organizational issues that you need to address to plan and hold effective meetings.

1. Frequency. How often a group meets largely depends on the number of problems needed to be addressed along with the complexity of the problems. If you are holding a meeting strictly for the purpose of communicating information, once is enough unless you run into problems that were not anticipated. If you plan on holding multiple meetings, meet at the same time and on the same day of each week to assure consistent participation.

2. Duration. All meetings should begin and end at a specific time that's rigidly enforced. Ideally, a single meeting should not last for more than two hours. You're better off holding multiple meetings than trying to cram everything into one long meeting.

3. Priority. At the outset, every meeting you hold should be assigned a priority. If you plan to assemble a large group of people, the meeting should have a high priority if for no other reason than what it costs to have all of those people attend, based on their hourly wage. Each member should assume full responsibility for their role in the meeting and they should have an assigned alternate in the event that they cannot attend.

4. Place. Meetings that are held in conjunction with lunches are seldom effective. One cannot eat and listen as well as a person who is not eating. Conference rooms with adequate seating are preferred meeting sites.

5. Agenda. Prepare your agenda for the meeting ahead of time. This will serve to inform meeting participants about the issues that will be discussed and who is responsible for key components of the meeting. Agendas can also address the purpose of the meeting so that everybody is focused on what needs to be accomplished.

6. Priorities. Establish a procedure for determining the relative importance of each agenda item. This can be done quickly at the start of a meeting with a simple vote on the importance of each agenda item.

7. Action items. There are four primary ways to dispose of an action item: 1) an acceptable solution has been reached, 2) the problem is delegated to an outside group for resolution, 3) the problem is delegated to an individual or subgroup for a recommendation of a solution to the group, or 4) the problem is removed from the agenda for whatever reason as long as a majority agree with the action. In no case should a problem be left hanging.

8. Notes. Don't record everything that anybody says in a meeting. It'll turn people off and you will get artificial answers to tough questions and issues. However, it is appropriate to document in summary form, what was agreed upon or not agreed upon in a meeting. E-mail summary remarks or conclusions out to all meeting attendants as a way to confirm group agreement.

Minutes of the meeting should be distributed or e-mailed to all participants as soon as possible after the meeting. At a minimum, the minutes should contain a summary of all decisions reached during the meeting, a record of the disposition of agenda items, and all task assignments that identifies who, what, and when.

(?) *Help: How to Hold Successful Meetings* (Career Press, 1997) by Paul Timm covers 30 action tips for managing effective meetings. You'll learn how to invite the right people to your meeting, develop a proper agenda, and how keep your meetings short and to the point.

Communicate With Stories

John Hansen is a colleague of mine who recently landed a president position with a multi-billion dollar corporation. As John was preparing to travel to the subsidiary locations and introduce his five-year business plan, he asked me if I knew of a non-offensive "icebreaker" joke he could use in his presentation. I told John the one about the new company president who asked his predecessor for some advice, as he was about to leave his office for the last time. "My advice to you is contained in a contingency plan that's in three sealed envelopes labeled one, two, and three. The first time you have a problem that you don't know how to solve, open envelope number one and it will tell you how to solve the problem. Use the other two envelopes in the same way but save them for as long as you can." He handed the envelopes to the new president who carefully placed them in the front drawer of his desk.

Several months later, the new president ran into a problem that he had tried to solve several different ways without success. In desperation, he reached into the drawer for envelope number one, opened it, and read, "Regardless of what the problem is, blame it on me and that will give you additional time to seek a solution." It was good advice and it worked.

A year later, he found a need to go back into the drawer for envelope number two to help him solve another problem. The message in the envelope read, "Reorganize. It will buy you at least another six months." So he reorganized and found that the advice was better than he expected. The reorganization not only bought him time but it actually resulted in some improvements.

A year after the reorganization, he found himself confronted by yet another dilemma that seemed to defy solution. In desperation, he reached for the third envelope. His optimistic expectations were shaken when he read the message, "It's your turn now to prepare three envelopes for your successor." When John told the joke, he got the desired laugh from his vice presidents by making himself the object of the joke, and built rapport with members of his staff.

The art of telling stories in good taste can do wonders when you are about to address a group of people in a tense setting. It accomplishes several important objectives. First, it immediately puts your audience at ease because laughter is what humans use to eliminate stress. A well-told joke or story helps level the playing field. Because you are the speaker, you are the perceived leader of the meeting. However, when you start the session off with a story, it helps your audience think of you as one of them. You gave them something to laugh at and they'll appreciate you for it.

? *Help: Simply Speaking* (Harper Collins, 1998) by Peggy Noonan is an audiotape that will help you polish your presentation skills and add substance to everything you say.

Become a Performer

In a recent public survey about fears, people were asked if they were more afraid of speaking in public or dying. Most people said they feared the prospect of having to stand up and speak to an audience more than they feared dying. And yet, your ability to speak effectively to a large or small group is one of the critical components that you will need to rely on to promote yourself.

Hosting a talk show is one of the oldest activities on television. A talk show friend of mine told me a talk show, just like a public speaking engagement, was nothing more than a performance. You may feel that because you're a business professional, the idea of becoming a performer when you make a speech is unsuitable for your speaking engagements. You may employ financial, industrial, and commercial idioms because that is the language you're comfortable with, but if you don't perform at your speaking engagement, nobody will listen to what you have to say. The very moment you rise to talk to an audience, step up to the podium, and open your mouth to speak, you become a potential performer. The more you can accept that notion, the more successful you'll be at promoting yourself. Here are six things that will help you perform better when you speak:

1. Don't hold the microphone if it's likely to shudder. Leave it on its stand.
2. Don't draw attention to your hands. If you must take a sip of water, make it as swift as you can.
3. Leave your notes on the table or lectern where you can refer to them as necessary. If your eyesight is poor, raise them as necessary and then put them down.
4. If one of your legs is trembling, shift your weight to the other leg. If both legs are trembling, move your feet back, lean forward, and grasp the table or lectern in front of you.
5. Avoid drinking anything with caffeine before you speak. Anyone who is prone to jumpiness can become hyped by tea, coffee, or cola before they speak.
6. If you are nervous, don't let your audience know it. The focus of your speech should be on its message and any indication of inadequacy won't help you get it across.

Have you ever seen a speaker who impressed you when they walked up to the podium, before they even said a word? When he starts to talk, people listen because the speaker is confident, informative, and everyone can understand what he's saying. A good speaker keeps the audience interested in everything they say and scores a comfortable laugh when it's appropriate. When they end their speech, everybody in the audience is impressed and thinking, "This guy is great. He's going to go far in our company." Most accomplished executives are excellent public speakers, which makes sense. Whenever you face an important speaking engagement, prepare yourself to make the best possible impression you can.

(?) *Help: Is There a Speech Inside You?* (Prentice Hall, 1994) by Don Aslett starts with the basics of what it takes to make a speech that's guaranteed to capture the attention of your audience.

Use the Power of E-mail

The power of the pen, or e-mail in this day and age, if properly presented, can be mightier than the sword. Or at a minimum, appropriately written words can directly influence which way the sword swings. Several years ago, IBM demonstrated how the pen controlled the swing of the sword. In the late 1980s, IBM was going through the wretched exercise of trying to reinvent itself like a lot of other corporations at the time and had endorsed the popular slogan of the day: "The customer is always right."

To reinforce IBM's commitment to its customers, CEO John Akers sent an e-mail to IBM's 425,000 employees telling them that if they encountered any customer-dissatisfaction issue, they could e-mail him directly with the specifics of the problem. When I first saw Akers' e-mail, I doubted if he could even begin to respond to a minimum number of customer problems. If only one out of every thousand employees sent him an e-mail once a week, he would be obligated to respond to 425 weekly customer-related problems.

At the time Akers' e-mail was sent, my IBM friend Dale was entertaining a schoolteacher from Flagstaff, Arizona who had come to Colorado for a week of vacation. During her visit with Dale, she mentioned a problem her school district was encountering with IBM. They had taken delivery of an IBM AS400 mid-range computer, but could not install the system because the power cable was missing. Their IBM representative told them there was a cable shortage and IBM was doing its best to locate one. The teacher went on to explain to Dale that the school year was about to start and her computerless district was getting desperate.

With the stroke of a keyboard rather than a pen, Dale fired off an e-mail to John Akers apprising him of the problem. As the story goes, Akers personally called the IBM representative in Flagstaff and said, "I understand you're having a problem locating an AS400 cable. I'll bet that I can find one within the next five minutes." That same afternoon, an IBM Learjet flew into the local airport where the cable was placed into the hand of a shaken IBM representative. The Flagstaff school district was up and running in time for the start of their school year, thanks to the power of e-mail.

⑦ *Help: The 3 Rs of E-mail* (Crisp Publications, 1996) by Diane Hartman and Karen Nantz show you how to get the most out of every e-mail message you send by using the right words.

Hook Your Audience

What allures, entices, captivates, and tantalizes a presentation? It's a hook. A hook is a statement that you use specifically to get attention. Hooks are dangled in front of you every hour of the day and night as you watch television, listen to the radio, read newspapers and magazines. Newspaper hooks are called "headlines." Television and radio stations call their hooks "teasers." Do you remember the hook in Wendy's classic television commercial that showed an old lady eating one of their competitor's hamburgers and said, "Where's the beef?" What a great hook!

A hook can be a statement or it can be an object that you use to get the attention of your audience when you're making a presentation. Use your hook in the beginning to get everyone's attention, and if they're properly used, they're an excellent way to capture the attention of an audience. A typical hook should be no more than a 30-second statement. Here are several questions to ask yourself to find a good introductory hook with zing:

1. What is the most unusual part of your presentation? Can you fit it into one sentence that has zing?
2. What is the most interesting and exciting part of your presentation? Can if fit into one sentence that has zing?
3. What's the most dramatic part of your presentation? Can it fit into one sentence that has zing?
4. What's the most humorous part of your presentation? Can it fit into one sentence that has zing?
5. Does the hook lead to the objective of your presentation?
6. Will your audience relate to the hook?
7. Does the hook relate to the approach you plan to take in your presentation?
8. Will the hook excite or interest your audience?
9. Will the hook fit in the front of your presentation?

Let's assume that we have come up with a great hook for a presentation that you are about to make. Your next step is to determine if your hook serves better as a statement or a question, because either format is acceptable. I prefer hooks that are questions whenever possible. The purpose of the hook is to get the attention of the audience and they'll usually pay more attention if someone asks them a question. Which of these hooks would attract more of your attention? "All great leaders share one common attribute," or "What one key attribute do all great leaders share?" Once you decide between a statement or a question, create your hook. If your hook is a question, you must provide the answer to the question immediately after you raise the question.

Here's an example of how to use a hook to tie your presentation together and capture the attention of your audience at the same time. Suppose that you're meeting with your senior managers to discuss the division's dismal profit performance. Your objective is to get the division back on a profitable track within three months. You know your management team is paranoid about making any decisions for fear that if they make the wrong decision, they may lose their jobs. Your approach is to get everybody involved in making the tough decisions necessary to restore profitability to the division.

Here's the hook that you use at the start of your presentation: "If you continue to sit back and rest on your laurels while this division goes to hell, how much longer do you think you're going to be here?" You've captured everyone's attention with the question hook. Now you quickly follow up with an answer that would assure the complete cooperation of your staff when you say, "If you don't start making the tough decisions you need to make now, you can kiss your job goodbye tomorrow. Here's what we're all going to do to solve the problem." Our hypothetical hooks relate to your objective, capture the attention of your audience, and motivate them to take action.

A hook can also be humorous, but it also must capture interest. Although some people believe that it's not appropriate to use a humorous hook, I disagree. If you're looking for the best response you can get out of your audience, then they have to be relaxed or they simply won't participate in any discussion. The use of a humorous hook at the beginning of a serious presentation can do wonders. Be careful about using jokes because you have too much at stake if the joke falls flat.

Sometimes the use of a visual hook rather than a verbal hook can do wonders for your presentation. Milo Frank was conducting a communications skills workshop at a major corporation where five managers made presentations to senior managers on how to get women on fast career tracks. Two chairs were set in the middle of the room with an empty pair of women's shoes placed under each. The opening statement was, "Where are the women who'll fill these shoes?" It was a great visual hook that complemented the opening statement. I saw an extreme version of a visual hook several years ago when I was attending a communications seminar about how to get people's attention. It was brilliant. As the speaker came out to talk, he took what appeared to be a spectacular fall on the stage. As he got up off the floor, he grinned and said, "Got your attention, didn't I?"

If you don't come up with some way to engage your listener's attention at the outset of your presentation, you'll cripple your main message. Keep track of personal experiences and anecdotes that may make good hooks by jotting them down in a notebook. You never know when they will come in handy when you're called on to make a presentation.

Eliminate Poor Communication Excuses

How many times have you been involved in a problem and when you ask the other guy what the cause was, he tells you it was because of "poor communication." In fact, poor communications is the one common component of every problem. It can be ineffective, divisive, and injurious to cooperative efforts. In many instances, people are forced to make important strategic decisions without the benefit of timely information, which has not been communicated to them. As you move up the corporate ladder, your assent and even your survival will depend on how you communicate to others and how well you nurture the communications channels that you must rely on. Let's take a look at some of the obstacles that negate effective communications:

✓ *Individual motives.* An individual's drives and motives within an organization can be extremely strong. If they do not share a common goal with you, their personal drive for achievement will mitigate their willingness to share information with you.

✓ *Rejection of ideas.* The rejection of ideas or decisions of others can occur because of an "I can do it better" mentality. A breakdown in communications occurs when that happens.

✓ *Hierarchy.* The greater the number of vertical structures there are within an organization, the more likely there will be a communication breakdown in the organization.

✓ *Organizational structure.* The different functions and divisions within an organization can become so autonomous and staunchly independent that lateral and cooperative communication becomes difficult.

✓ *Performance appraisals.* Most performance plans are designed to reward people for their individual achievement. There is no incentive for them to openly communicate beyond their respective realm of influence.

Although it may be difficult or impossible for you to influence or change some of the communication barriers that may exist within your organization, there is one area that you can influence. A surprisingly prevalent reason for a lack of communication comes simply from the fact that people do not know who to contact when they need information. Effective communication begins with knowledge that is supported by knowing who knows what. You have to know who to contact when you need more information. Chances are, you may not know the right person to contact but you know somebody else who might know who to contact. That is where your network becomes a critical support tool in the communications process.

(?) *Help: Verbal Advantage* (Audio Renaissance, 1997) is an excellent audio book by Harrington Elster that helps you add new and vital words to your vocabulary to improve your ability to communicate in any situation.

Make Outstanding Presentations

Top-flight executives and leaders in every business and profession all share one key ability: They know how to present themselves, their ideas, and how to get their points across. It's always a pleasure to watch a good speaker and listen to their perfect choice of words and controlled tone of voice. We watch their easy and commanding stance, their sophisticated use of body language as their head turns to everybody to show that every member of the audience is important to them. If you have the opportunity to make a presentation to a large group of people in your organization, you can, in a relatively short period of time, make a lasting impression, which would have been impossible to duplicate on a one-on-one basis. Here's why:

Suppose you have been asked to make a 15-minute presentation at an executive staff meeting that will include 20 department and division heads. You produce an outstanding presentation that receives a standing ovation. Look what you've accomplished. In a short period of time, you have impressed your company's key decision-makers. Who will they be thinking about when the next promotional opportunity comes up?

Being a skillful presenter takes a lot more than preparation and practice. Good presenters also possess certain qualities. Do you have these qualities? Review the following list and put a check mark next to the ones you possess. While no one person will meet all of the points, a successful presenter will make a continuous effort to improve upon their presentation skills. Here's how:

Control. Skillful presenters always control their presentations, regardless of internal or external disruptions.

Knowledge. It's not only important for presenters to know their presentation material, they must also be perceived by the audience as being very knowledgeable about the subject they're addressing.

Awareness. Good presenters knows where they're going in their presentation at any one moment in time. They can sense how their presentation is being perceived by their audience and will subsequently change course (that is, reiterate a point) if they sense confusion in the audience.

Tactfulness. Tasteless comments or jokes undermine any presentation. Tactfulness is an important trait of all good presenters.

Responsiveness. Depending upon the setting, presenters welcome questions from their audiences. They're quick on their feet to give precise and meaningful answers to anybody's question.

Persuasiveness. Most presentations are designed to get an audience to think or act in a specific way. Good presenters are persuasive throughout their presentation.

Enthusiasm. Good presenters are willing to accept the fact that they are entertainers to some degree. They subsequently exude high-energy enthusiasm for the topic they are discussing in a manner that excites their audience.

Directness. If a presentation deals with an unpopular or controversial subject, good presenters are willing to step up to the table and share their honest and often controversial feelings with their audiences.

Flexibility. Professional presenters avoid being too rigid on any one issue. They do not want to alienate their audiences or stifle interactive communications.

Possessing all of the important qualities of a good presenter are definitely important, but they can get lost if your delivery is not there. Delivering an interesting, powerful presentation requires more than reciting what you have rehearsed and being an expert in your subject. It requires constant coordination of content, the use of dynamic voice delivery techniques, and audience interaction.

Always Look Good

In any face-to-face communication between two or more people, messages are communicated not only through words, but also through body language, the underlying dynamics of what is not said. Body language is the looks and moves you make with the various parts of you body to either reinforce and strengthen your words or contradict what you have said.

Michael Deaver used to manager President Reagan's news conferences. Deaver had Reagan stand in front of the open doors of the East Room for press conferences because it made the President appear livelier and more substantive. He told reporters, "The open door with the light coming across the halls makes a much better picture of the President." Margaret Mead once told President Carter, "It doesn't matter what you say. What's important is how you look." In the business world, the same rules apply. Is the boss seen as too cold and too far removed from the troops? If he's going to spend the day out in the plant, why not wear work clothes and a hard hat to set a positive body language image. Never underestimate how the strength of image projection can move people and supplement or disrupt your promotional objectives.

The story about my friend Bill Mitchell offers a classic example of how the improper use of the way you look can destroy your promotional opportunities. Bill was the chief financial officer (CFO) for one of Phillip Morris' subsidiary companies in California. Bill has an MBA from Columbia University and is infinitely qualified to be any company's CFO. Because the subsidiary company didn't fit into Philip Morris' line of business, it was sold off and Bill was replaced by the acquiring company's CFO. In other words, Bill was out of a job.

He came to me for advice on how he should mount his executive search campaign. I told him, "Bill, you have to shave your full beard and mustache off if you want to improve your CFO image. Like it or not, the finance execs that will be interviewing you typically have very conservative tastes." Bill quickly discounted my comment and told me, "If they won't accept me the way I am, the hell with them."

Although I empathized with Bill's comment and tried to convince him that he could always grow his beard back after he landed a position, he was still bent on ignoring the image part of body language. A year later, Bill was still looking for a job and in fact, he hadn't even gotten an offer. Fortunately, he had saved enough money to ultimately buy a small business, keep his beard, and run it the way he saw fit. Your basic appearance is of course not the only way to establish you image through body language. Here are several other examples of how body language techniques are used:

- ✓ **To praise someone's comment.** Raise your fingers to you lips and kiss them as you flick you hand away from your lips.

- ✓ **To show you're thinking.** Clasp you hands with both thumbs pointed up and touching, place in front of your chin as you look up at the ceiling in deep thought.

- ✓ **To show what you think about a bad idea.** Place you forefinger against your temple and rotate it.

- ✓ **To show disagreement.** Tug on your earlobe with the finger of one hand.

- ✓ **To show that you are alert.** Place your forefinger alongside your nose.

Thousands of books have been written about communicating with appearance and body language. People spend their entire lives studying it and asking others how to use it. Although it's not that hard to learn how to use body language effectively, you don't just reach out, grab it, and tell yourself you are now an expert at using body language. You have to acquire it the old fashioned way, a little bit at a time. As you begin to use more effective body language, things will begin to go more smoothly when you communicate with others and your self-confidence will grow. Your accomplishments will increase along with your ability to communicate, and before you know it, you will have created a self-perpetuating machine where everything you say to others fuels your enthusiasm.

? *Help: Body Language in the Workplace* (McGraw-Hill, 1991) by Julius Fast shows you not only how to use body language to make your point, but also how to read the body language of others so that you are in a better position to influence their thinking.

Speak With Vision

In his book *Presentations Plus* (John Wiley & Sons, 1992), David Peoples contends that 75 percent of what people know comes to them visually, 13 percent from hearing, and 12 percent through smell, touch, and taste. Because human beings are visually oriented, presentations that include visual aids such as slides and graphics create impressions that are more lasting than the corresponding words. Information that is seen has a much greater chance of being remembered than information that is heard.

Whenever possible, paint a picture so that your audience will understand exactly what you're trying to communicate, even if you have to do it verbally. I recently attended a dinner party sponsored by the Society for the Prevention of Cruelty to Animals (SPCA). The society's president delivered an excellent message when he created a vision that was the theme of his speech: "Imagine yourself alone and starving. You're on a cement street surrounded by cement buildings. The buildings have no doors or windows. The street is endless and there is no hope. That's what a lost or abandon cat or dog faces when it's turned loose in the city."

When you're communicating, you want your listener to see as well as hear what you're saying. Descriptive words that relate to a story help listeners visualize what you're talking about. For example, here are two sentences that basically say the same thing. Which one would you choose:

1. Deficits have a bad effect on the economy.
2. Deficit spending is spreading, and like a poison, it's devastating our economy.

The first sentence is dull and boring. It leaves no picture in your mind as to what is happening. I added only four more words to the second sentence that includes two action verbs to paint a picture of what's really happening. It should have been easier for you to listen and assimilate what I said in the second sentence because there's color in the sentence. You can visualize what is happening through the words. Imagery words are useful in all types of daily communications.

How many times have you heard the boring words from the airline stewardess, "Please keep your seat belts on until the plane comes to a complete stop." I remember one stewardess said, "If you'd like to not suffer the embarrassment of falling down in the aisle, please keep your seat belts fastened until the plane comes to a complete halt." Her added comment got a good laugh and the passengers stayed seated.

The use of descriptive words helps you paint a picture for your listeners. Words create images, and whether you're talking about a dog, the budget deficit, or seat belts, you can make your message colorful, interesting, and memorable with imagery. Using imagery in a message is one of the most enjoyable parts of making a presentation because the very process forces you to be creative.

Idea: It's hard for some people to smile even though a smile conveys our upbeat attitude about our life, while our frowns project the opposite. When we greet others with a smile, we take the first step toward showing our value and worth to that person. Keep smiling and you'll promote yourself a little more every time you smile.

Help: Just Say a Few Words (M. Evans & Co., 1988) by Bob Monkhouse is filled with great ideas on how to effectively communicate and speak with vision to both small and large audiences.

Chapter 6

Networking Yourself to the Top

Company social functions offer you a unique opportunity to meet all kinds of power players who could influence your promotion. You can attempt to meet people either by standing in a corner to see how many execs will move over your way or by taking a self-directed approach to meet the people you need to know. If you watch a typical office party, you'll notice that those who have power usually arrive late and seize a corner for themselves. Those who are unsure of themselves tend to stand by the door or at the bar to make sure they are in the traffic flow where they can at least be noticed.

Regardless of the fancy antics that are played at company functions, they offer you with an excellent opportunity to network your way in with the people you need to get to know better in order to achieve your promotional goals. In this section, I'll cover four basic techniques you can use to expand your network of strategic contacts. I'll also show you how to effectively work large and small crowds, what to say, and how to maintain your network once it's established.

What's a Network?

Networks were once thought to be television stations like ABC or CNN until business networks were introduced. A business network is an organized collection of personal contacts that you can rely on when you need help or information. Networking is a technique in which you connect people you know with people they don't know and they do the same for you. "I'll show you mine if you will show me yours" is one of the hidden rules of networking. You network to build relationships that will help you in some aspect of your promotional campaign.

You may meet a person who at the outset may not have a direct fit into your plan, but your intuition tells you this person is worth knowing. That's reason enough to build the relationship. You do that by not asking, "What can they do for me today?" The proper network technique to use is the reverse question where you ask, "What can I do for this person today?" If you turn it around and consistently put other people ahead of what you want from them, you'll develop super relationships that even Superman can't break apart.

When you start building a network, meet as many people as you can to get your volume of contacts up. Initially, it's okay to have almost too many contacts because it doesn't hurt to practice on your introduction hooks, but you will soon discover that it's not easy to keep in contact with a lot of people. Networking is a contact sport. If you can't contact everybody in your immediate network at least once a month, your network is too large. Have you ever gotten a call from someone you haven't heard from in more than a year and after they told you how much they missed you, they asked you for a major favor? How did you feel? Used? To avoid becoming a user, you must be able to contact everyone in your network on a routine basis.

As you develop your network, get choosier about whom you'll allow into it. An ideal network will include people who can help you expand your center of influence. Because of your respective personal relationship, they know exactly what they can do to help you and vice versa. For example, if someone in your network meets the executive director of a professional association and they know you want to make a presentation at its annual meeting, they'll call you and tell you the executive director is expecting your call. That's how good networks function.

Warning: When you are with a group of people, don't confuse charisma with a loud voice. In order to establish a lasting relationship with people, you must first be prepared to give them something to entice them to join your network.

Natural Systems

Take yourself out of your current job for a moment and let's assume you own a farm, which is the sole source of your livelihood. Consider how ridiculous it would be if you didn't follow the farming system. You forget to plant in the spring, play golf all summer, and then try to get all of the planting done in the fall so you have a fall harvest. Because farms are natural systems, a consistent process must be followed over time if you want to reap the rewards of what you sow. No shortcuts are allowed on the farm or any other natural system for that matter.

These same principles apply to networks, which are also natural systems subject to the laws of the harvest. In the short-term, you can get by and make a favorable impression by exercising your charm and pretending to be interested in other people. Eventually, the challenges of life will cause your true motives to surface and your short-term relationship will disappear because you didn't take the time to understand the people's personalities—learn what turns them on, what turns them off, and what motivates them.

Had you taken the time to sow motivation into your relationships outside the company, your relationships would have had long-term staying power. How many times have you thought of someone whom you haven't seen for months or even years? What makes you think of them? It was probably because in your past relationship, they had a way of motivating you and you were subsequently always up when you were with this person.

? *Help: Nobody to Somebody in 63 Days or Less* (Applied Business Communications Inc., 1996) is a great guide on how to quickly build a business network and use word of mouth to advertise your capabilities.

How Networks Have Evolved

A few years ago, organizations were structured to be self-contained units where everybody had clearly defined roles. Their level of structure, definition, order, and their internal processes were all routine and understood by anyone who was assigned to them. Today's millennium organization is very different. Hierarchy, definition, and order have been replaced with fluid, organic, and dynamic structures that are capable of instantly responding to the changing needs of the organization. Jobs at all levels are no longer defined by a set of impersonal and technical work tasks. People's performance is judged by their ability to adapt, reflect, and respond to lightning fast changes where their success depends on how successful they are at developing their networks.

Building and managing a network is not only key to getting yourself promoted, it also supports you personally. According to Webster, a network is a structure of cords or wires that cross at regular intervals and are secured at the crossing. Although the human side of networking is not a precise science, they do involve making connections between people and groups. And what you will require out of your network will undoubtedly vary, depending upon your personal goals. You may use it to meet with your peers for advice on how to achieve your promotion goals or you may use it to solidify key steps you need to take to get promoted.

Most people have used networks at some stage of their careers to aid in their advancement. Your first high school summer job may have come about because you or your parents knew someone who had an in where you wanted to work. As you grew older, you developed more sophisticated networks to enhance your career objectives. This traditional and well-tested means of advancing your early career has become even more important as organizations become flatter, which allows for fewer promotional opportunities. In today's organization, knowing how to network to advance your career is an essential survival skill.

Who you know is still important. Your current contacts are the raw material for your network. They in turn have their own contacts, which have their own contacts, and so on. What you have at your disposal is the potential of an enormous network. Organize the raw material of your network into a database using index files, computer records, or whatever suits your style. Even if you love your job and have no intention of moving on, start developing a network database now. The perfect time to do it is when you don't need it. Here are several ideas that will help you get started:

1. The more you exercise your networking muscles, the stronger they get, and the easier networking becomes.

2. At end of every network conversation ask, "Now what can I do for you?" or "How can I help?" A relationship formed to meet the needs of both parties on an ongoing basis is critical to building a network.

3. Always be positive when you hold a network conversation by offering help, thanking your colleague for a favor they may have done for you, or offering some needed information. Avoid making negative comments that include offering gossip.

4. Great networks are two-way streets. If you're just a receiver, you'll fall out of whatever network you think you belong to.

5. Network as if your professional life depends on it, because it does.

6. Why aim low when you seek to find members for your network? How you start your network will help determine when you'll get promoted.

7. Go to every association meeting and trade show you can to find candidates for your network. Sign up for work committees that offer you an opportunity to build your internal network organization.

8. Remember the names of everyone you meet. Write them down on network cards that you carry in your pocket. In addition to their name, include their job title and telephone number. Over time, add personal information, such as birth dates, family member names, education, affiliations, and special interests.

9. Don't be afraid of the "no" word when you ask someone to join your network. It's the second best answer there is because at least you know where you stand.

Your network isn't the only network you should get to know inside and out. Get to know your boss's network too. Everybody has their own kitchen cabinet. When the people your boss listens to become part of your own network, you are following the right crowd.

? *Help: How to Work a Room* (Warner Books, 1989) by Susan RoAne teaches you how to introduce yourself, how to accumulate contacts, how to become an active listener, and how to polish your manners when entering a roomful of strangers.

Develop Your Relationships

Developing solid relationships with the right people is critical if you expect to move up the corporate ladder. Relationships will be key to your success, not just because of what other people can do for you, but because you learn when you're around the right people. Good relationships broaden your perspective on life, keep you informed about what's going on, and refine your ability to listen and communicate. All of that is the lifeblood of the promotional process.

When you become conscious about professional relationships and know how to select people who can help you, you may have to dump some of the excess baggage you've been carrying around in your network. That may include people you may have known for a long time, but who have stopped contributing to your professional life. Maintaining relationships is a time-consuming process and quite frankly, you may not have time to nurture old relationships. If you want to get to the top of the ladder, you have to be selfish with your time. There are essentially three types of network relationships. They are:

1. Sinking relationships. This type of relationship is like a dead weight that will either drag you down, hold you back, or sink you altogether. It's a relationship with a person who has low esteem and who is often avoided by others like the plague. The fact that you are seen talking to them can even place a cloud over *your* head. They're often called "chicken littles" who believe that the sky is about to fall in at any moment. Whenever you meet with them, they will tell you what's wrong with anybody, from the janitor on up to the CEO. They'll tell you the company's about to go out of business, the food in the cafeteria is rotten, electronic bugs have been planted in the bathrooms, and so on. Get rid of these types of relationships as quickly as you can, or they will sink you.

2. Floating relationships. As the name suggests, a floating relationship acts like a life raft. If you should fall into the swamp, their life raft is always there to save you. They're the ones you trust and with whom you can vent your frustrations in order to purge your system. In most floating relationships, you don't expect to get any viable advice other than a few kind words like, "Yeah, that's a rough one. I don't blame you for being pissed off." That's okay because this type of relationship provides you with an important escape valve for your emotions that you don't want to demonstrate in front of someone who can influence your promotion. By definition, floating relationships usually have only a minimal direct influence on your promotion.

3. Power relationships. This type of relationship provides the power that will help accelerate your ascent up the ladder. All power relationships belong in your inner circle of influence for this reason. When two people get together in a power relationship, they are instantly surrounded by a sphere of energy where they tap each other's best ideas, invent anything, and drive each other's inspiration to its highest level. Power relationships can be professional or personal. They always generate such a powerful exchange of information that the relationship becomes the conduit for your creativity and bring out the best in you.

Any of your relationships can bounce around between the three types that we discussed. For example, some adverse event, such as a job loss, hits a person that's in your power relationship sphere and you suddenly have a sinking relationship to contend with. Do you drop them just because they have fallen onto some bad times? Yes! If that sounds harsh, then step back and consider the personal consequences you'll suffer if you continue to maintain sinking relationships. Don't let any relationship sink you.

Your Top 10 Guns

The core of your inner circle of influence should be made up of 10 people you can count on. Your top 10 can include friends, family members, and those with whom you have close ties in your professional world that all fit within our definition of power relationships. They are on the inside because they bring out the best in you and they want you to succeed because they know you want them to succeed. There's no competitive threat, they will never talk behind your back, and they'll always have your best interest at heart. It's a joy for you to be around them and it's a joy for them to be around you. If all this sounds great, then you are probably wondering why we restricted this beautiful group of people to 10? It goes back to what we said earlier. Power relationships deserve at least one contact a month, so 10 may be all you have time for. Just make sure you can maintain a solid relationship with whatever number you pick to be in your power relationship circle.

I also recommend that you maintain relationships with at least 15 people who can back up your top 10 power relationships. This group can be composed of both floating and alternate power relationship types who all share one common attribute. They are constantly broadcasting to the world how great you are because they believe in you. Yes, the group can be larger than 15 as long as you can maintain regular monthly contacts with them either by phone, fax, group meetings, e-mail, or correspondence.

Here's why you want to build back-up relationships. They act as your private radio show because they're always transmitting good stuff about you every day through their own respective networks. They also act as radio receivers collecting information from a variety of sources that they pass on to you. You may need them to replace a front-line power relationship member in your network. Suppose one of your key power relationship members retired and move to the Australian Outback. Where would you find a replacement? The most likely place to find a candidate would be in your back-up group.

Get Culturally Connected

Unfortunately, in most organizations, you can't get promoted if you're not culturally connected. I recently had lunch with a truly remarkable executive in his early 40s with an MBA from Stanford. Steve knows how to make the right decision almost ever time, and he was a contender for the CEO position at a well-respected Fortune 200 company. Although the current CEO told him he's a contender, he's not! I know it, Steve knows it, and the CEO knows it. Why not?

Steve focused all of his energies on getting promoted to CEO when he first joined the company five years ago. He took over a struggling division and was given a year to make it profitable, or it would be shut down. He succeeded by increasing sales fourfold and profits tenfold. His performance was so superior to his peers running other divisions that the CEO felt that he had to at least include him on his list of CEO successors. He now realizes he won't get the job because his style doesn't fit into the corporation's culture. He deliberately chose not to join the culture, which cost him the promotion.

Corporate culture is the corporation's perceived way you should look, act, and perform to fit into the mold of the company's perfect employee. In this pinstriped company, Steve wore sports coats to work while his peers wouldn't be caught dead in anything other than three-piece suits. He was noisy. They were sophisticated. He's an entrepreneur that can make it on his own. They were autocrats who checked with the CEO before making any key decisions. The bottom line of the story is that it doesn't make any difference how good you are. If you don't fit into your organization's culture, you won't get promoted.

Put Sizzle in Your Answers

People who are trying to build networks will always ask you, "What do you do?" If you give them a "ho hum" answer like, "I'm a manger at IBM," you've just lost an opportunity to connect with the person you're talking to. A more appropriate answer might be, "I manage a group at IBM who develops surveillance software for our military spy satellites. I also ride horses, play lots of tennis, and love to write books." In 15 seconds or less, I have added not only sizzle to my answer, but offered the other person an opportunity to pick up on several subjects that may be of interest to them. When they respond with, "Oh, you like to write? So do I," your networking conversation is off and running. Following are some other ideas that will help you put sizzle in answers:

Be memorable. Offer something about yourself that's memorable. For example, "My name is Dave Rye, as in rye bread" helps people remember my name by way of association. It's corny, but it works!

Float to the top. It does not matter how far down on the food chain you are when you start a networking conversation. You'll begin to eat better if you offer answers that show you're on top of the world.

Follow the rules. If there is any single networking rule to follow, it's not, "How can I get the other person to do something for me?" Rather, it's, "How can I do something for the other person?" If you're answering a question, add some more sizzle with a follow-up question: "What can I do for you?"

Answering questions with sizzle is great if you have an opportunity to converse with a person who you want to get into your network. However, we are sometimes confronted with gatekeepers. Gatekeepers are people who typically answer the phone to screen calls before they'll allow you to talk to whomever is behind their gate. Get to know the top dog's gatekeeper if you want to get into the compound. This can take several calls. Following is an example of how to get past a gatekeeper by using some sizzle.

Let's assume you want to arrange a meeting with Mr. Larson, the CEO of a company you're interested in joining. Your first call gets you to his receptionist who you do not know. She answers, "Mr. Larson's office. How may I help you?" You reply with, "Good morning, my name is Dave Rye. Whom am I speaking with?" The receptionist gives you her name (Joann) and you ask her some nebulous question like Larson's e-mail address. When you place your second call and Joann answers the phone, you respond with, "Joann, this is Dave Rye. We talked briefly the other day. I need your help." You have positioned your pending request with a personal note, which should get you a favorable response like, "What can I do for you?" You say, "What do I need to do to get an appointment to see Mr. Jacobs?" and you are on your way.

Idea: How many people have you known, including yourself, who happened onto a chance meeting with someone who changed their lives? Perhaps the meeting led to a new job, a friendship for life, new business opportunities—all because of a chance meeting. Never pass up an opportunity to meet new people.

12 Networking Mistakes to Avoid

Have you ever gone to a potluck party and everyone brings great home-cooked dishes to the table except for the nerd who shows up with a package of napkins? He's also the same person who's always saying, "Gee, I wish I could have a party like this. I just don't have the time. By the way, could you do me a favor?" If you think you can get by on your charm and good looks when you network, you're sadly mistaken. It's great to be liked but it is even greater to be needed. Following are 12 networking mistakes that you never want to make.

1. Don't build a network that looks just like you. Diversify so that you can benefit from the thoughts and ideas of people who may have opposing views from yours.

2. Don't assume your credentials entitle you to exercise power in your network. I don't care if you are the president, CEO, and chairman of the most powerful corporation in America. Everybody in your network should be on an even playing field.

3. Don't confuse visibility with credibility. Peacocks are beautiful birds that have learned over time that they can draw attention to themselves by strutting around with their feathers cocked to draw attention to themselves. The same antics don't work for human strutters. If you want to turn people on to you, show them what you know.

4. Don't answer for the other guy. Always avoid the temptation of trying to answer a question someone may ask an associate in a multiple conversation. If you do, it condescends the authority of your associate and places you in the disadvantageous position of being the "know-it-all."

5. Don't overdraw your account. Although I've said it before, I'll say it again: Always give more back to your network that you receive.

6. Don't be a stiff. When one of your network members helps you in a big way, buy them dinner or do them a favor in return to show your appreciation. You'll receive more kudos than you can imagine for the small price of your reciprocation.

7. Answer your calls. Okay, you're not in, and one of your network members left you a message. Call them back in a reasonable period of time if you want them to stay in your network.

8. Get your phone to ring and your e-mail message volume up. One of the best quantitative measures to determine how well your network is working is to track the number of inbound calls you get from your network members. The more calls you're receiving, the better your network is working.

9. Don't underestimate the value of personal touch. Two of the most powerful words in the English language are still "thank you" and "please."

10. Don't fake it. If you don't know the answer that someone is asking you, tell them you don't know. If you know someone who may have the answer they're looking for, offer them a referral name or call the referral on their behalf.

11. Never assume a junior person is not worthy of being in your network.

12. When you're networking, learn to distinguish between information and gossip.

According to best-selling business book author Harvey Mackay, "The riches of the world pale in comparison to the value of an honest opinion." Other people's opinions of you have an enormous impact on your promotability. Your network is one of the best and most credible reflections of your talents.

Warning: Don't play the numbers game. Networking is not a numbers game where the idea is to see how many people you can meet and business cards you can collect. Any fool can do that. The object of the game is to compile a qualified list of people you can count on when and if you need them.

Stay in Touch

Bill Clinton was the first Democratic president to be reelected since Franklin Roosevelt, a feat that he attributed largely to his network of friends. A *New York Times* reporter asked him what he did to maintain his network of political contacts. He told him, "Every evening before I turn in, I list every contact I made that day on 3 x 5 cards, with vital statistics, the time and place of the meeting, and all other pertinent information for my network database that my secretary maintains for me. My friends have served me well over the years." How true! Following are 10 ways to stay in active contact with everyone in your network.

1. Use your calendar creatively. Record special days that are important to your network members, such as birthdays and anniversaries. Call them, or at a minimum, send them a card to let them know you're thinking about them.

2. Observe organizational changes. Anytime one of your network members gets promoted or moves to a new organization, congratulate them on their advancement.

3. Use your business trips constructively. If you take a trip that brings you geographically close to a strategic network member, offer to meet with them for lunch or dinner. Put the tab on your company's expense account.

4. Get e-mail. If you don't have an e-mail address, get one or you'll quickly become obsolete in the communication world.

5. Call your members when they're down. When you hear of a problem that any member in your network is having, call them immediately and offer your help. It's the best way to show your support.

6. Let you network members know of any major changes in your situation. If you're going on vacation, call them and ask if there is anything they need before you leave.

7. Be there at important functions. I don't care if there are going to be hundreds of people who show up at an important function of one of your network members, such as their promotion party or their daughter's wedding. If you're not there, they will know it. Show up!

8. Turn your network at least every 90 days. Challenge why every member of your network should remain in your network at least every 90 days. Networks have a tendency of getting stale and if you're not periodically replacing or adding someone in your network, your network is stale.

9. Become a gateway of information for your network and organization. Always be on the lookout for information that the various members of your network could use. Make it a point of sharing any information you receive on a regular basis.

Competition within networks can be a healthy thing as long as it's done in good taste. There is nothing wrong with the members in a network vying for popularity and recognition. It is an indication that the creative juices are flowing and everybody is on their toes to produce for each other.

Warning: Nothing can be accomplished until you begin, which can be a serious weakness with many people. They'll always trying to put things off, such as building a network, until later. When you decide to build a network, get it started now rather than tomorrow when you'll never have enough time.

Always Be Positive

I can't think of too may physical handicaps that would be worse than being blind *and* deaf as a baby. It happened to Helen Keller. From a very young age, she was never able to see the faces of her mother or father, or even hear the basic words, "I love you" each night before she went to bed. Can you imagine the frustration she felt as she was growing up not being able to express how she was feeling or what she wanted. It was only through the commitment of her mentor, Anne Sullivan, that Helen was gradually able to communicate. Although she never regained her sight, through her spoken and written words, she inspired millions and built a worldwide network of admirers. Throughout her life, Helen harbored no bitterness or resentment and fulfilled her destiny of always being positive.

Although you will not find the word "positiveness" in the dictionary, it best describes a critical element that you will need to establish a top-notch network. It's made up of two components: 1) a positive attitude and 2) fulfilled relationships. Having a positive attitude as opposed to a negative attitude is the stuff that rubs off on anyone you touch in your network. They meet you, you talk to them, and because you are predominately a positive person, they feel good about the relationship they have with you.

In the process, you build better relationships, which over time become fulfilled relationships. Fulfilled relationships are long-term relationships that you establish with people whom you can count on if you need them. Most likely, they are an integral part of your strategic network. Zig Ziglar summed it up when he said, "Your success is directly proportional to the number of people you make happy and successful." In his book *Zig Ziglar's Secrets of Closing a Sale* (Berkley Books, 1982), Ziglar identified several ways to do that within a network environment:

Respect. Mutual respect is the foundation upon which any relationship must be built. If respect does not exist on both sides of the relationship, there is no relationship. Lots of things enter into the respect side of a relationship including trust, confidentiality, and integrity.

Needs. We often get so wrapped up in our own daily routines that we either ignore or fail to see the needs of others. Responding to the needs of others is the catalyst that's used to build relationships. You can respond to the question, "Hey Dave, can you help me?" two ways: "I'm busy right now" or "I'm busy but let me see what I can do to help."

Security. A fulfilled relationship is covered with a security blanket. It's a relationship where you can confide your deepest secrets to the other person and feel secure that they will be safe. You've got someone you can talk to where you can share your private thoughts, feelings, and needs in a secure environment.

Admiration. Have you ever heard someone say, "I don't care what they think"? Deep inside you intuitively knew that they really did care or they wouldn't have made the statement. We all have an innate desire to be admired by others. Mutual admiration is the cement that holds relationships together.

Communications. One of the biggest roadblocks to building strong relationships is the inability to communicate effectively. Clearly, you can't develop a relationship if you don't understand what the other person is saying either verbally or in their body language.

Resolution. Conflicts will arise in any relationship. You have a choice of either resolving the conflict or dissolving the relationship. You'll invest a significant amount of your time to build a lasting relationship. You can lose it in a second to an unresolved conflict.

Criticism. If you're perfect, you don't need criticism. For the rest of us, criticism is the stuff we rely on to improve ourselves. When someone asks you, "What do you think?" have you ever said "It's just great" even though you thought it was lousy? You didn't want to hurt the other person's feelings. Honest opinions must be in place for a lasting relationship to work.

Display your positive attitude by always saying something nice to everyone you meet. Sincere flattery can go a long way to pave the road to your success. We all know what it feels like when others say something nice about us. Take the initiative and share that same feeling with everyone you meet. Words like, "You have a beautiful office" or "That's a great tie you're wearing" will often do it. If you don't know what to say, try "It's great to see you." You'll be amazed at how much more responsive people will be to you when you first say something nice, even if you are meeting under adverse conditions.

Idea: What's in a handshake? When you're on the receiving end of a weak, clammy handshake, you feel like shuddering and getting as far away from this person as you can. In contrast, a firm handshake conveys contact, self-assurance, and warmth. If you have a weak handshake, get rid of it and replace it with a firm handshake that conveys your friendliness to others. A weak handshake will not help you get promoted.

Help: *Power Networking* (Bard Press, 1992) by Sandy Vilas covers the whole menu of how to strategically use a network to increase your power within an organization. If you need more help on learning how to set up a network, read Dena Michelli's book, *Successful Networking* (Barrow's Educational Series, 1997).

Use Your Networking Time Wisely

Ben Franklin once said, "If you save your pennies, watch the dollars grow." The same principle applies to time in a reverse relationship. "If you waste minutes, you'll lose hours." And I don't need to remind you that every minute or hour you waste can never be replaced. How many times have you heard your friends and associates say, "If only I had more time. I should have done it then." Networks are time-consuming entities to build, so as you pursue your networking goals, learn how to use your time wisely. It will pay you back in big dividends throughout your career. Let's look at several ways you can improve your use of time when you're building a network.

Think about the minutes. A minute is nothing, right? There are 1,440 minutes in a day, most of them insignificant. So what if you throw a couple of them away. They're insignificant because you're looking at the big picture. You'll watch the lengthy hours rather than the minute minutes. Good luck if you plan to make some serious inroads up the promotional ladder. Next time you schedule a meeting with an executive, see if they tell you, "You've got a couple of hours so you can make your point." Their more likely response will be, "You've got 10 minutes to convince me that your idea is worthwhile."

Plan your day. Are you the type of person who walks into work in the morning and mentally announces to yourself, "When the stuff hits the fan, I'll handle it on a first-in, first-out basis." Do you assign the same priority to everything you do during the course of a day? If you do, then be prepared to severely limit the promotional level you'll be able to achieve. Leaders know how to identify their priorities on a daily basis, at the beginning of each day to leverage their use of time.

Don't let your time get stolen. You're in your office working on a critical project that's key to your promotional plan. Just when you think you have the solution to a major technical problem that has been plaguing the project from its conception, your phone rings. Reluctantly, you answer the phone only to be reminded by your buddy about your luncheon date, and because she has nothing to do at the moment, she proceeds to tell you about her nephew's wedding on Saturday. You've just been robbed of 20 minutes plus whatever time it takes to recover your problem-solving frame of mind before the phone rang. If you're working on something important, never allow anybody to disrupt you and steal your critical time.

Avoid urgent requests that aren't urgent. We often allow urgent requests, those events that demand our immediate attention to disrupt the time we have allocated to work our priorities. Urgent requests for your immediate attention typically come from a ringing phone. "Sam just turned in his resignation and if you don't talk to him before he leaves the building, he's gone." Assuming that Sam is an employee you don't want to lose, you would probably be better off allowing him to leave the building to "cool off" before you talk to him. With the exception of real emergencies, most "urgent" requests do not require your immediate attention.

Don't procrastinate. Procrastination in the ultimate waster of time. If you're a procrastinator, then you have adopted the motto of putting off everything that's important until the last minute, when you don't have any time left. You'll find yourself welcoming any urgent request for your time because that's the justification you need to postpone a priority assignment.

Taking control of your time is a relatively simple thing to do, and yet most people do not do it. Why? Because they do not recognize the importance and value of their time and they do not know how to do it. If you don't control the use of your time, you will seriously jeopardize the time you need to devote to building your network.

Warning: Do it now. Nothing gets accomplished until you start. Why do some many people religiously practice Murphy's Law #301: "Always put off today what you can do tomorrow"? Tomorrow never comes and it's one of the best friends of a procrastinator. Put "eliminate procrastination" at the top of your self-improvement list. Then write down all of the things you know you should have done but haven't done because of procrastination. Then do them!

💡 ***Idea:*** You may be tempted to rush into new ideas and programs at the expense of other things you should be doing to assure your promotion. Practice moderation. Moderation reminds us that great accomplishments are made when objectives are reached by a well-thought-out process.

❓ ***Help:*** *How to Make the Most of Your Workday* (Career Press, 1994) by Jonathan and Susan Clark shows you how to organize and manage priorities. You'll also learn how to work smarter in the process.

Become a Most-Wanted Person

Are you pulled between the urge to slow down and your fast drive to get promoted? Are you frustrated because no matter how hard you try, there is still a big gap between where you are and where you really want to be? Are you avoiding personal problems staying at work rather than going home and facing the music? Are you clinging to an obsolete work ethic that says if you're not suffering from overwork, you are not succeeding?

Whatever your reasons may be, it's time to get rid of the excess baggage of constantly overwhelming yourself with work. If you keep on running at a fast pace, you won't have time to pay attention to what you need to do to get promoted. Working hard and not smart will not get you promoted, so don't even think about going there. Chances are you haven't had time to pay enough attention to the people who can help you get promoted.

The true measure of how you're doing at getting yourself promoted will be determined by the number of leaders who know you because you've taken the time to develop relationships with them. When this happens, you will be amazed at the things that will begin to happen. All of a sudden, you'll get invited to key strategy meetings because one of the leaders you know believes you have something to offer. They'll start calling you for advice and opinions on difficult subjects. You'll be wanted. All of that injects adrenaline into your promotional campaign. Here's what you need to do to become a most-wanted person:

Acknowledge people. I realize that you are already doing this, but I want you to go even deeper in your acknowledgments. Any chance you get, compliment or acknowledge people. "What a great presentation, George" or "I like your idea. Can we discuss it?" are two examples of acknowledgements. When you tell people what they want to hear, they love it and will support you whenever they can.

Help people develop themselves. When you help people develop themselves, you help them fill a space that they desperately want to fill. You do this by helping them get rid of their excess baggage. "George, what do you mean you don't think the Executive Review Board is going to buy your recommendations on the Thompson Project? Let's make sure they do. Come over to my office and I'll help you put your presentation together." If you know you're going to need George's help getting access to his boss, a key figure in your promotional campaign, you have just solidified his support by helping George.

Show people where their strengths are. Just as you're reading this book to help you develop your promotional strengths, use what you know to help others develop their strengths. Be honest and tell them where you think they are "short changing" themselves and what they can do to improve.

Actively solicit advice from people you respect and listen to what they have to say, even if you disagree with their comments. People love to be asked to give their advice on just about anything. When you allow people to give you advice, you open up the opportunity to develop a personal relationship that you can count on to support your promotion.

? *Help: Successful Negotiating* (Career Press, 1998) by Ginny Pearson Barnes gives you all the necessary information to become an expert negotiator and a most-wanted person in the process.

Idea: The people who work for you don't care how much you know about them, only how much you care about them.

Chapter 7

Teaming to Win

I recently spent two days with five executives of one of the nation's premier computer companies. Although the company is a 600-pound gorilla in its field, it has undergone many recent organizational changes, including bringing on a senior vice president (Jim Hanson) from the outside to direct the activities of the five execs attending my seminar. All five had been in their jobs for less than six months and didn't really know their boss, the new senior vice president.

Prior to the retreat, Jim had concluded that this group was not working well together as a team and sought ways to improve the situation. He hired me to assist him in resolving the problem. We agreed to accomplish two objectives over the two-day session: 1) Clarify how things are currently working between the execs in his divisions, and 2) Clarify how things should be working in a team environment. Once I was able to convince Jim's five direct reports that they had an opportunity to excel in their careers by pooling their talents and information together rather than trying to outshine one another, the team came together.

Historically, teams were thought of as one-shot deals. You identify a problem, get a bunch of people together to brainstorm possible solutions to the problem, pick one solution, implement it, and the problem goes away. The team celebrates its victory and disbands. Not anymore! Teaming has matured to take on a more global approach. Entire divisions and even entire companies are considered one team by CEOs, complete with team goals and objectives that everyone in the organization is chartered to develop. Your ability to direct the activities of successful teams will supplement your promotional objectives nicely.

Do It As a Team

When people are promoted, they often rush out and grab the reigns of their new organization to make a flying start at solving all of the perceived problems in their organization. Understandably, their initial concern is to justify to the superiors who promoted them that they made the right selection. After all, what is a leader for if they can't show positive results the moment they take charge?

Unfortunately, rushing in to take charge is a good way to cut your promotional efforts short. Leaders who are eager to produce quick reforms, instant cures, and dramatic increases in productivity succumb to the "new broom" mistake. They assume there is a mess that was left over by the previous leader that they have got to sweep up. In the process, they end up creating their own mess that often gets them terminated before they ever really get started. Successful leaders enlist the help of individuals in their organizations to solve problems by building teams and, in the process, their organizations as well. Following are seven reasons why:

1. It's easier for team members to identify with organizational goals if they participate in implementing those goals.
2. Team members develop a greater feeling of control over their lives, which frees them from the fear of a leader's arbitrary abuse of power.
3. When a team participates in solving a problem, they learn a great deal about the technical and management complexities it takes to reach an acceptable solution. They learn from each other as well as from the team leader.

4. Participation on a team provides opportunities for team members to satisfy many of their higher-level needs for self-esteem and acceptance within the organization.

5. Teams help break down status differentials between team members and management, which fosters more open communication in the organization.

6. Teams enable management to exemplify the kind of leadership behavior they want the members to learn to support the organization. In this way, management philosophies can be more easily moved down through the organization.

7. Higher-quality decisions often result from bringing into play the combined resources of team thinking.

In your current position, learn how to become a problem-solving facilitator by either forming or participating on work teams. It will make your job much easier than if you try to solve all of your organization's problems on your own and you'll enjoy a lot more recognition as a team player. It's also a key factor to your promotion. You must know how to get your subordinates to learn how to solve many of their own problems so that you're free to manage and lead your organization.

(?) *Help:* Peter Capezio's *Winning Teams* (Career Press, 1998) walks you through the process of getting people of varied backgrounds to work together to obtain a mutual goal. It also discusses how successful teams achieve top results by utilizing the individual contributions of each team member.

Become a Keeper

Collaboration is one of today's most revered management styles. With the call of leadership philosophies whirling all around us, the most critical and effective decisions are being made in a collaborative setting rather than by a single person. More than ever, people huddle together in a team environment to make strategic decisions because there's a common belief that two or more heads are better than one.

Unfortunately, some people make a career out of just sort of being there when they're involved in a collaborative meeting. They'll just hang around and blend into the landscape while everyone else is diligently trying to come up with solutions to tough problems. One exec told me, "They're not keepers." He went on to explain: "A keeper is like a fish that you have just hooked and you don't want it to get away. They are the people who attend meetings and always make a vital contribution to the meeting. Keepers are people who like to make things happen, whose ideas, and opinions are sought out by everybody in the meeting."

You've seen keepers in action before when your boss says, "Be sure to run this idea by Sue first to make sure she backs it. Check with Tom to see if he anticipates any problems." Keepers are master collaborators because they give way more than they receive. They seize the initiative to offer what they know and thus have avoided being left out of the power circles of influence. That's why they always rank high on the promotion list.

Write down two occasions over the past year when you sat idly in a meeting and let someone else speak up with an idea that was similar to the one you kept in your head. That person got credit for your idea and you got nothing. Next time, speak up when you have something to offer. Look around your organization and find a project that's about to start. Don't wait for an invitation. Jump in and volunteer your ideas that will assure the success of the project. If you make it a habit of doing this, you, too, will become a keeper. As more of your contributions become noticed, you will expand you inner circle of influence, and accelerate your opportunity for a promotion.

Idea: Being proactive in motivating others is a critical element in inspiring superior team performance. When you can get your team to dedicate itself to unselfish trust and work toward the good of the organization, you are ready to get promoted.

You're Ignorant. So What!

In the old days, if you called someone ignorant, it was considered a grave insult because it was one step away from being called a moron. Today, ignorance typically refers to that lack of knowledge in a particular area or field. It's common practice and often desirable for us to own up to our own ignorance. However, some people get wrapped around the connotations of the early definition to their detriment and refuse to admit to any lack of knowledge. They ignore their own ignorance.

Avoid this pitfall at all costs because it will not serve to benefit your promotional ambitions. A person who refuses to admit that they don't know everything can become so underdeveloped that they'll act with bloated ambition and become know-it-alls. They'll refuse to acknowledge to their associates that they are inexperienced or don't know all of the facts about a new undertaking because they think that to do so would be a personal flaw. Because they want to get promoted, but sense that they aren't getting anywhere, they pretend to know everything. Know-it-alls assure their own failure because their depth of knowledge exists only in their mind and as a result, their associates tend to ignore them. They will bristle or go into withdrawals if anyone tries to help them, so people just avoid them in general.

It is much more healthful to your promotion efforts if you are willing to share your ignorance. There is no shame in admitting that you don't know something you need to know. To make sure you don't get trapped into the know-it-all box, take out a piece of paper and jot down five instances when you have recently claimed that you knew more than you did. If one or two of these instances were calculated bluffs that worked out in your favor, that's okay. Anything beyond that will jeopardize your performance and career.

List five areas of ignorance that you need to share with trusted friends. Ask them to make up their own list on your behalf. Do the same thing for them and compare lists. You'll discover that they may identify an area of ignorance that you are quite adept at but for some reason, have not successfully demonstrated your knowledge in. Look for areas where your associates can help you and you can reciprocate by helping them.

Idea: Ask not what your teammates can do for you. Ask what you can do for your teammates. If your teammates know this, they will follow you wherever you want to take them.

Warning: There is nothing that helps people's conduct through life more than their knowledge of their own characteristic weaknesses. You must also be capable of recognizing other people's weaknesses so that you are in a better position to handle bizarre situations when they occur. For example, if a manager with the power tells you to do something that's wrong, what will you do? The quickest way out of the illicit encounter is to simply do what you are told. In the short run, that approach will get you to first base. But you'll never make it to home plate with a boss who now expects you to be the implimenter of all her illicit demands.

Teaming With Mr. Nice

Everybody loves nice people, but if they are too nice, they can drive you crazy. Anything you ask them always generates a favorable response like, "Great idea" or "Yes, yes, yes." They'll say yes to anything to avoid using the negative "no" word. I once worked for an exec (Gene) who was one of the nicest guys you'd ever want to know. I had a great idea that I was sure would enhance my career. When I asked Gene what he thought about my idea, he said, "Great idea. We ought to implement it. Send me a proposal." I'd work my backside off preparing the proposal and a week after I submitted it to him, he told me he hadn't had time to review it yet.

After several months of "I haven't had time to review it yet" excuses, I abruptly realized that it was Mr. Nice Guy's indirect way of telling me he really didn't give a damn about my idea. If he had been capable of saying no in the first place, he could have saved me a lot of work and aggravation.

Unfortunately, we all have to deal with Mr. Nice Guys at some point in our career. They can effectively stop you from doing something that's important to your career as I illustrated in my episode with Gene. The challenge is to get them to do what they say they will do. Following are several ideas that will help you pin down Mr. Nice Guy and get a commitment that you can count on.

Qualify their "yes" answer. You know in advance the answer to your request is going to be yes, but that's not the answer you should be looking for. You need to find the answer to the "when" question. When will they approve the implementation of your idea? When I asked Gene the "when" question three months after I first got my go-ahead, he told me, "Sometime in the future because it's not one of my top priorities right now." Bingo! If I had asked the "when" question up front, I would have at least known that my idea was not one of Gene's top priorities.

Pretest your idea. Where does your idea fit within the priority scheme of things? You can't answer the question until you first know what the priorities are. Determining what different individuals perceive are the priorities within an organization can be a difficult challenge. Here's why: Priorities is another word for problems. Organizations love to use the word "priority" because it sounds so much better to say, "We're working on our priorities" as opposed to saying, "We're working on our problems." The problem is that high-level priorities are usually not widely publicized within an organization. If you have an idea that is designed to solve a problem, you need to first find out where the problem fits within the organization's priority list. To test the validity of your idea, first find out how important the problem it will solve is to the organization.

Probe with questions. The answers you get to carefully worded questions are essential to qualifying the importance of your idea when you are dealing with Mr. Nice Guy. For example, let's assume you have an idea that will eliminate the high rate of turnover that is occurring in the sales department. You believe that this has got to be a priority problem within the organization. Before you present your idea for a solution, you ask the question, "Gene, as we all know, we are experiencing high rates of employee turnover in our sales force. Is this a major problem that we should address?" If he says yes, you have prequalified the importance of your idea.

Ask for a commitment. Asking Mr. Nice Guy to make a commitment is substantially different than asking for a "yes" response. A "yes" response carries no weight in time, whereas a commitment does. When someone makes a commitment, they are essentially placing their word and reputation on the fact that they will do specific things in a specific time frame. For example, you ask Gene this question: "If I submit a proposal to you next week, when can I expect either your approval or rejection?" Note the fact that I worded the question to solicit either a "yes" or "no" response. A "maybe" response doesn't cut it! If you get a response like, "Sometime before the end of the month," you have a commitment. If you get an "I don't know" response, you are back to square one with Mr. Nice Guy.

If you're willing to step up to the challenge of building a relationship with the nice guys in you life, you can substantially strengthen your network of reliable people. That's because most of the nice guys will be outside of the networks of your competitors who haven't figured out how to reel them in. As a final note, when you deal with people who only know how to offer "yes" answers, ask probing questions to qualify their answer and find out what's really going on within the organization before you introduce the full depth of your idea.

Avoid Pessimists

In Disney's classic movie *Cinderella*, little Gus the mouse said, "If you don't have anything nice to say, don't say anything at all." Gus was talking about pessimists who never have anything nice to say. They're totally negative about everything, including themselves, and believe in the worst scenarios of the Murphy's Law: "Whatever is right, will go wrong and whatever is wrong will never be right!" They have no inhibitions about letting others know how they feel and use the big "no" any chance they get. "I've tried it and it won't work" is one of their classic responses.

Pessimists are not fun to be around and are experts at destroying even the most optimistic of personalities. They are not conducive to helping you pursue your career goals so avoid dealing with them as much as possible. However, there may be extenuating circumstances where you are either forced or required to deal with a negative person. Maybe they're your boss, a peer that you need support from, or a subordinate that you can't afford to lose. Your challenge when dealing with a pessimist is to get them to move from a fault-finding attitude to a problem-solving attitude, or in modern terms, from stagnation to innovation. How do you do that?

Remember when you were struggling through high school algebra and the instructor tried to convince you that if you added two negative numbers together you ended up with a positive number? You never understood why but you accepted what she told you just so you could pass the final exam and go on to bigger and better things. Forty years later, I finally figured out what the instructor was talking about. If a pessimist makes a negative statement and you counter with a positive statement, the negative person becomes more negative in their beliefs.

If, on the other hand, you counter their negative response with your own negative response, you can instantly become aligned with a pessimist and subsequently open up the door for a solution. For example, you might say, "I agree with your adverse position, Sue, based on my similar negative experience. Now, let's discuss what we can do to solve our problem."

Pessimists can become invaluable resources to supplement your career objectives if you use their skill-sets to your advantage. For example, suppose you have a great idea that you know intuitively will work if you can identify all of the problems you'll have to overcome to implement it. That's when you want to present your idea to a pessimist. They will be quick to tell you everything that can go wrong with your idea. Listen carefully to what they have to say. You can always discount any problems they present that in your opinion are not relevant, but chances are they'll identify problems you hadn't thought of.

Idea: Dr. William Mayo, founder of the famous Mayo Clinic, once said, "Lord, deliver me from the man who never makes a mistake, and also from the man who makes the same mistake twice."

Become a Team Leader

Not too long ago, *The Wall Street Journal* published an article by United Technology Corporation. It read: "People don't want to be managed, they want to be led. Whoever heard of a world manager? World leader, yes. Educational leader. Political leader. Religious leader. Scout leader. Community leader. Labor leader. Business leader. They all lead. They don't manage. The carrot always wins over the stick. Ask your horse. You can lead your horse to water, but you can't manage him to drink. If you want to manage somebody, manage yourself. Do that well and you'll be ready to stop managing and start leading."

Effective teaming has become a critical component of just about every modern organization. It's how they inspire their people to address the tough issues and challenges of the day. Your ability to form, develop, and lead teams is an essential credential for your promotion, particularly if you're working for an organization that actively supports teaming concepts. I know of several people with outstanding credentials who work for tea-oriented companies and were not team players. They never got promoted. When they ask me what they should do, I tell them to either learn to become a team player or join a company that doesn't like teaming.

All teams need team leaders. They don't need team managers. Your ability to become a good team leader is one of the most important steps you can take in assuring the success of your team. What are the differences between a manager and a leader? A manger administers, maintains, and plans. A leader innovates, develops, and sets direction. This is not to say that you cannot be a strong manager and leader at the same time, which is what you should be striving to accomplish. Harvard business professor John Kotter said, "Most U.S. companies are still over-managed and under-led today. However, with careful selection, nurturing, and encouragement, dozens of people can play important leadership roles in a business organization." Following are eight leadership traits you should strive to develop to become a team leader.

1. *Vision.* A team leader must be able to develop a vision, a mental image of where he or she wants the team to go that's in the best interest of the organization. The vision has to be effectively communicated to every member of the team to assure that everybody is on the same page.

2. *Scope.* Team leaders have to be able to see the big picture or the team's mission to effectively lead. They understand what the short-term and long-term ramifications are if the team does not accomplish its mission.

3. *Innovate.* A great team leader is not afraid to step out on the edge of anything and make innovative decisions. The development of innovative ideas and thinking is one of the primary reasons why teams are formed in the first place.

4. *Focus.* Good team leaders remain focused on the missions of their teams. They know how to identify their

major objectives and are not diverted by minor issues. They control the direction of the team rather than allow something else to control it for them.

5. *Rational.* During the closing minutes of the 1978 Gator Bowl, Woody Hayes, one of the top coaches in the country, ran onto the field and punched one of the opposing players who had just made a key interception. Ohio State fired him the next day. Leaders who can't control their emotions should not be team leaders.

6. *Pressure.* Forming a team to tackle critical problems and issues invites pressure. The pressure can take many forms that include meeting tight deadlines, working long hours, and accommodating the multiple personalities of the different team players. Good team leaders know how to handle pressure.

7. *Teach.* A leader demonstrates their willingness to give to others by teaching them anything they know. In a team environment, teaching becomes an important factor to help assure that everybody on the team is operating at approximately the same level.

8. *Involvement.* A team leader knows how to coax the quieter members of the team to participate in team discussions. They do this by encouraging all team members to present their opinions and ideas.

The quality of the team leader on any business team will help shape the degree of success the team will enjoy. Leadership qualities are inherent in some people while in others, they must be learned. If the seeds of experience, imagination, and innovation take root in an individual, then they have the capacity to grow into a leader. As Vince Lombardi once said, "The strength of a team is in the strength of its leader."

Idea: You don't become a leader just because you say you are one. It's much more dependent on what you do rather than what you say. "It doesn't matter how well you're leading if no one's following" Harvey Mackay wrote.

Build an Awesome Team

How you select people for a team is more important than how you manage them once they're on the job. If you start with the right people, you won't have problems later on. If you select the wrong people for a team, you'll find yourself in serious trouble. You'll have to rely on all of the revolutionary management techniques to bail yourself out. It's often difficult to find top team players if you have to rely on bogus references, professionally designed impersonal resumes, and canned interviews. Here's a checklist to follow when you're searching for team members:

- ✓ **Find above-average people.** Why take the time to train an average person if you can get an above-average person who already knows what needs to be done?

- ✓ **Develop a profile.** Before you start your search for team members, develop a profile of what a perfect member would look like complete with educational requirements, work experiences, ability to communicate, and motivation levels. Check every candidate against your profile to get the best fit.

- ✓ **Avoid learning curves.** Team assignments usually have short completion time lines so you don't have the luxury of conducting extensive training sessions for team members. Make sure everybody on the team is equipped with the basic knowledge to get the job done.

- ✓ **Network.** Use your internal network to find outstanding candidates. A referral from a highly regarded member of your network is 10 times better than taking in someone you don't know.

- ✓ **Ask everyone: Why do you want to be on my team?** Dismiss anybody who gives you a nebulous answer like,

"I don't know" or "Because I'm a team player." You're looking for people who can demonstrate a specific interest in what the team has been assigned to accomplish.

✓ **Schedule duplicate interviews.** Ask one of your trusted associates to interview candidates that interest you. Get their independent opinions to see if they validate your opinion.

✓ **Ask similar questions.** Ask all candidates the same basic questions so that it's relatively easy for you to compare the different responses.

After you have selected your team, make sure every team member understands the mission of the team. Candidly talk to them about the challenges the team faces and the time lines that are involved. Teams who believe that a problem can be solved tend to get busy solving it.

(?) *Help: Team Building: An Exercise in Leadership* (Crisp Publications, 1992) by Robert Maddus shows you how to find the best and most qualified players for you team. He also shares his ideas on what to do to keep your team motivated.

Keeping Your Players Motivated

There are literally thousands of different ways to motivate people. For obvious reasons, I won't attempt to cover them all here. In fact, I'm only going to cover one that I got from *Sports Illustrated* when one of their editors interviewed Fran Tarkenton, one of the greatest quarterbacks in the history of football. During the interview, Fran recalled a play he called where he had to block. Blocking quarterbacks are about as rare as three-dollar bills. His Minnesota Vikings were losing to St. Louis and Fran knew that he had to call a surprise play to save the game. Nothing would surprise the defense more than if he became a blocker. The play worked when Fran took out a tackler and his teammate scored the game-winning touchdown.

Bud Grant was the Viking coach at the time and when he came into the locker room after the game, Fran was waiting for his expected pat on the back. It never came. Everybody involved in the play was praised by Grant except Fran. Fran confronted Grant in the privacy of his office and asked, "You saw my block, didn't you, Coach? How come you didn't say anything to me about it?" Grant replied, "You don't need it. Yeah, I saw the great block you made. Fran, you're always working 100 percent out there. I figured I didn't have to tell you." Fran replied with, "Well, if you want me to block again, you do!"

The moral of the story is don't ever take any of your winning team members for granted as Bud Grant did with Fran Tarkenton. If you're a team leader, you keep your team motivated by touching each of your players at least once a day with praise and words of encouragement. If someone on the team is slipping, jump in and say, "What can I do to help?"

(?) *Help:* If you get a chance, read my book *1,001 Ways to Inspire Your Organization, Your Team, and Yourself* (Career Press, 1998). It literally includes more than a thousand ways to inspire and motivate people in all different kinds of business settings.

Idea: As the legendary Alabama coach Bear Bryant once said, "Winning isn't everything, but it sure beats whatever is second."

Join Joint Ventures

Anytime you get a chance to participate in a joint venture, do it. Joint ventures between organizations to form strategic alliances have become extremely popular in recent years. They represent the highest level of mutual cooperation between two or more entities within a company or between companies to accomplish a common goal. Participating in joint venture activities can do wonders to your promotional prospects by adding valuable contacts to your network, while openly displaying you to a wider band of decision-makers outside of your immediate work domain.

Joint ventures are typically formed between organizations to attack a common business problem or to take advantage of a unique business opportunity. Insight Enterprises in Tempe, Arizona was experiencing a high turnover rate in its direct sales force that was costing the company millions in recruitment, training, and productivity expenses. A joint venture task force was formed involving participants from every department within the organization to resolve the problem, and it was resolved. If you have the opportunity to participate in a joint venture, learn how they work, and what you can do to make sure you're a positive force in the venture.

Companies will sometimes form joint ventures to use their respective technologies to develop new products and services. IBM needed corporate partners to test its new chip technology on microcomputers and subsequently formed a joint venture alliance with Apple Computer and Motorola. Although there are a number of factors that make joint ventures attractive to senior management, they usually center around competitive, technological, or administrative challenges.

In most cases, any man or woman who participates in a successful joint venture stands out like a rising star. Almost all joint ventures are initiated by executive management so there's a lot of skin in the game. You can chalk-up an incredible number of points and even a subsequent promotion if you're a key player in a successful joint venture. Even if the venture fails for reasons that were beyond your control, and you did everything in your power to prevent its failure, you'll still earn points. Let's look at some of the reasons why some joint ventures can fail:

Shotgun approach. Unfortunately, a lot of joint ventures are formed with the greatest of intent, but little regard is expended on who should participate in the venture. Management, in their ultimate wisdom, decides to throw a bunch of people at the venture with little regard as to who's qualified or not qualified. As one CEO put it, "It's like throwing a bunch of flies on flypaper. Those who are able to get off the paper will be the ones who'll make it work." Unfortunately, a joint venture that gets started using a shotgun approach usually gets swatted down in the early stages. Stay away from these kinds of ventures.

Suspect goals. If a joint venture is to work, all of the participants must know exactly what the goals are and they must be 100-percent committed to the venture's goals. If the goals are unclear or each side is suspicious of the other's motives, the venture is destined to fail. This type of problem becomes very apparent at the outset of a joint venture and can be quickly solved if senior management is willing to step into the venture and clarify all goal-related issues. If they're not willing to do this, you run the risk of being set up in a venture that will go nowhere.

Win-lose mentality. Joint ventures depend upon reciprocity and the sharing of scarce resources between all the participants who collectively see it as a win-win opportunity for everybody. The lack of a perceived bilateral benefit can lead to mistrust and a feeling of exploitation by team members. A win-lose mentality develops that will undermine the entire venture. In most cases, it's up to the venture participants to resolve this problem within their own ranks.

Incomplete information. The foundation for the success of all joint ventures relies on each side knowing its own strengths and the offsetting competencies of its partners. If the partners in the venture knowingly withhold key information from the venture because they are suspicious that the other participants are doing the same thing, the outcome of the venture will be severely compromised. If mutual trust and respect cannot be established when the venture is first formed, it will fail.

It should be clear to you by now that coordination, cooperation, and effective communications are the critical ingredients to ensure the success of a joint venture. In fact, those same three ingredients are required to ensure the success of anything from a personal to a business relationship. If you can help bring them all together when you participate in a joint venture, you'll jump at least two notches up the corporate ladder.

(?) *Help:* *The Practical Guide to Joint Ventures and Corporate Alliances* (John Wiley & Sons, 1989) by Robert Lynch shows you how to organize joint ventures, how to select the right people, and how to assure their success.

Idea: It is a rough road that leads to the heights of greatness. "When you come to a fork in the road, take it," Yogi Berra once said.

The Sky Is Falling!

If you remember your nursery rhymes, Chicken Little was always running around the barnyard yelling to the other farm animals to run for cover, fearing that the sky was about to fall. All of the animals would run for cover. Over time, they finally realized that Chicken Little didn't know what he was talking about and learned to ignored him.

I use to work with a chicken little who drove me crazy with his perception of perceived problems. The typical conversation would go something like this: "Dave, drop everything you're doing. We've got an immediate crisis on our hands that's going to require your full attention." Nine times out of 10, there was no crisis or even the hint of a problem. But in the interest of keeping the boss happy and my promotional opportunities alive, I'd go through the necessary motions to work on some invisible crisis. It was frustrating because it prevented me from working on the things I should have been doing to get ahead.

What causes chicken-little behavior? Perhaps they're the Rodney Dangerfields of the business world. They feel they "don't get any respect." To counter this nagging concern, they create crises to bring immediate attention to themselves and hopefully reinforce the fact that because they identified the crises, they deserve respect. You'll often hear them say, "Nobody around here cares" or "If I don't do it, it won't get done." Here are several steps you can take to help neutralize the chicken littles on your team and keep your career on track at the same time:

Get their attention. When someone is operating in the chicken-little mode, they've lost control of their better judgment and are highly emotional. You've got to get their attention. You may have to raise your voice and use caution words like, "Hold on, let's consider what you just said" or "Have you considered the alternatives?" Wave your raised arms slowly as if you were in the middle of a train crossing attempting to stop a freight train. If you're dealing with an aggressive chicken little, you may have to wait until they settle down before you try to get them to consider the reality of the situation.

Show concern. The last thing you want to do is tell or insinuate to a chicken little how ridiculous their perceived crisis is. Make sure your tone and language are friendly as you try to get them to inject reality back into their thought process. If you listen closely to what they say, you can usually learn what caused their concern in the first place. Ask leading questions like, "How did you learn about this problem?" Once you know what the cause of their problem was, you're in a much better position to diffuse the situation.

Stay calm. Whatever you do, stay calm when you're confronted with a highly emotional chicken little. Your calm interaction can act as a catalyst to dampen their excited behavior. You will know when you are on the right track when they start stuttering. Rapidly blinking their eyes or scratching their head are other indicators. That's a clear indication that their rational mind is beginning to catch up to their emotional mind.

If you're forced to interact with a chicken little on a recurring basis, you need to develop a long-term solution to the problem. You can't afford to have this type of person constantly disrupt your career plan. Remember, chicken littles are insecure people. If you can afford the time, offer them your ideas and thoughts to correct their problem.

Get the Most Out of Your Team

The era of pompous executives who set policy, delegate everything, and sit back waving their hands to wait for something to happen are over. We're now living in an era of hands-on employees where everybody from workers to management are responsible for making good things happen in a team environment within their respective organizations. Here are seven ways to get the most out of your team:

1. Shorten lead times. Challenge the amount of time people tell you it takes to complete a task, introduce a new product, or resolve a problem. It used to take Honeywell four years to introduce a new thermostat until someone challenged the system. Why did it take so long? A "Tiger Team" was assigned to the task of shortening the time frame. They cut it down to a year and every team member was rewarded with a promotion.

2. Encourage innovation. You don't have to rely on your company's employee suggestion program to get people thinking about innovative ideas for your organization. Even if you don't have a budget for prize money, your personal recognition will get you all of the innovative ideas that you want.

3. Get it right the first time. Nothing will bring you more adverse publicity than when you mess up on a major assignment. Test everything yourself if necessary to make sure it has been satisfactorily completed before you officially announce that your team's project is complete.

4. Beat the schedule. If you're given a team assignment that has a deadline, encourage the team to beat the schedule. Your boss and everybody else directly or indirectly associated with the project will be impressed.

5. *Make your buddies consultants.* Establish a business network with you close associates so that you can call on them if you need advice to solve a particular problem. Unlike commercial consultants, they don't cost you anything and because they know you, they have a better idea of your needs than a consultant who knows nothing about you.

6. *Keep an eye on quality.* Not every product is sold on the basis of its quality, but if yours is and your quality starts to slip, you're dead. If you lose your quality reputation, you've got about as much chance of restoring your reputation as you do getting the wind to stop blowing in the next hurricane. Cadillac thought it could fool its customers when it came out with a downsized Cadillac built on a Chevy chassis. That fiasco cost them millions.

7. *Recognize that failure may be the price you'll pay for learning how to get the most out of your team.* Philip Morris has suffered overestimating the marketing abilities of their General Foods acquisition to underestimating how aggressive Budweiser would be when their Miller Beer division was about to capture the nation's number-one beer spot. In spite of their failures, Philip Morris keeps getting up off the floor to try again and again as they learn from their mistakes. Maybe that's why they're still a Wall Street Blue Chip company.

(?) **Help:** *Teaming By Design* (Irwin Professional Publications, 1995) by Donna McIntosh-Fletcher shows you how to consistently get the most out of any team effort.

Idea: Ben Franklin once said, "We must all hang together, else we shall all hang separately."

10 Ways to Turn Your Team Off

Remember the old saying, "It's not only what you say to your team but how you say it that counts"? If you are trying to make a point, and your voice is soft-spoken or squeaky, you'll lose your credibility and probably your audience at the same time. Always deliver your presentation to your team with confidence mixed with a healthy blend of humility. No one likes to listen to an arrogant speaker in a team environment. If you can make your teammates feel comfortable with you and your communication style, you'll win their admiration every time. According to the National Speaker's Association, the 10 worst ways to turn people off when you talk to them are:

1. Using a monotone voice.
2. Reading your material if you're making a presentation.
3. Sounding boring and uninteresting.
4. Overusing "uh," "um," "they say," and "you know."
5. Lack of preparation including unorganized material, rambling, and becoming sidetracked.
6. Nervous habits such as fidgeting, swaying, and using annoying body language.
7. Speaking too long or going into overtime.
8. Repeating over and over again.
9. Not making eye contact.
10. Not relating to the audience or soliciting audience participation.

Effective communication is critical in a team environment. When you speak, you are usually addressing more than one team member, so it's essential that you adjust your communication style to accommodate the different personalities of all the team members. As a rule of thumb, you are generally making short, concise statements to get your point across and following up with questions like: "Does everyone understand what I just said?"

Idea: You cannot manage men and women into battle but you can lead them.

Chapter 8

Managing Your Way Through Minefields

Purveyors of the corporate rat race will tell you that character assassinations, back stabbing, and a variety of other political infighting tactics are, unfortunately, a normal part of corporate life. Nobody is naive enough to believe that these negative human relationships do not exist in the corporate world. In fact, they compete for a share of each day's activities in areas that may range all the way from the restroom to the boardroom.

Let's assume for a moment that your personal life is in some sort of upheaval and the last thing you need to contend with are pressures from work. As a result, you are not seeking out new opportunities or volunteering for initiatives because you don't want to risk encountering more personal conflict than you already have. If you take this approach, you make yourself a victim of low expectations. The key to your success is not to ignore conflict situations, but rather to control and manage them when they arise. In this chapter, I'll talk about what you can do to get people who get in your way out of your way as you climb up the corporate ladder.

The Evolution of Leadership

The word "leadership" didn't even enter into the English language until the early 1800s and even then, nobody knew what it meant. It took another 100 years before social scientists undertook serious studies about the phenomenon of leadership. It has only been over the past 40 years that researchers have been able to make up for the lost time by studying how people become effective leaders. Many of their studies provide amazingly consistent findings about what constitutes the characteristics of a good leader. They are summarized as follows:

1. A leader listens with understanding, is always willing to discuss problems, and is open to any new ideas.
2. A leader offers support and help. You can count on them to back you up when you need them.
3. A leader knows how to use the team approach to solve difficult problems. They are excellent facilitators of cooperation.
4. A leader avoids close supervision and is not a micro-manager. A leader does not dictate or rule by the book.
5. A leader is not afraid to delegate authority and they'll rely on other peoples' judgment because they have faith in the creativity of others.
6. A leader communicates openly and honestly. You can trust what they say.
7. A leader brings out the best in the people who work for them and is in constant touch with their people.
8. A leader is constantly working toward increasing interorganizational cooperation.
9. A leader is always on the lookout for ways to increase productivity, reduce costs, and increase profits.
10. A leader knows how to plan and set goals that people can relate to.

Leaders are born, not made. That's what most of the social scientist thought before they started their serious investigation of leadership 40 years ago. Back in the old days, when strong social class barriers made it next to impossible for anyone to become a leader, it appeared as though most leadership was inherited. If your name wasn't Rockefeller, Firestone, Rothchild, or from some other favorite family, you were not destined to become a leader. As class barriers crumbled, it became obvious that leaders were coming from all strata of society and it became common knowledge that leadership required much more than being born into the right family. Effective leaders are the ones who get promoted.

Warning: Effective leaders are not workaholics. If someone tells me they are consistently working 60-plus hour weeks, I will ask them why just so I can hear the "canned answer" of every workaholic: "That's what it takes to do my job." Then I tell them, "You're doing something terribly wrong. List 20 things that make you work that hard and I'll bet you 10 of them are nonsense." Workaholics are doers and not leaders. Former Time-Warner CEO Dick Munro said, "I'm dead against workaholics. Working like that causes you to lose enthusiasm and vitality, and it inhibits creativity.

Idea: Delegating is one of today's premier management styles. Even with the call of leadership whirling all around us, with record profits being reported by Wall Street, many of the critical decisions and most effective actions taken are a result of delegated assignments. More than ever, upper management is beginning to realize that if they cannot effectively learn to delegate even critical functions, they will be forced to confront a two-pronged problem. First, they flat out don't have the time to be effective leaders and second, if they can't delegate, then they may have the wrong people working for them.

Become an Exceptional Leader

The Wright brothers had a vision of air transportation and even though they were ridiculed, they were committed to making their vision a reality when their handmade aircraft took off from a dirt field in Kitty Hawk, North Carolina. Leaders who possess vision will relive excellence again and again. They'll repeat positive experiences, learn from their failures, and then move up to the next rung on the corporate ladder.

Exceptional executives are both excellent managers and leaders. Managers organize, schedule, budget, and administrate. Leaders inspire, create commitment, act as role models, and evoke the highest level of commitment they can from not only their subordinates but from everybody they touch. Exceptional leaders induce people to feel a reverence toward them because of their ability to inspire others. Here's how you can become an exceptional leader:

Be a visionary. A visionary is someone who can see possibilities that others ignore. They have a vision of what the future can be and they are committed to making it happen.

Develop an evolved ego. A person who has an evolved ego spends a great deal of time and energy trying to project a certain image that's not phony. At the height of his fame, Albert Einstein was asked, "How do you feel knowing so many people are always trying to prove you are right?" Einstein replied, "I have no interest in being right. I'm only interested in discovering whether I am right or wrong." Leaders with highly evolved egos do not need to prove that they are always right. Here's how they do it:

Be responsible to people. Exceptional leaders bring out the best in people by giving them enough autonomy to do their own jobs effectively, which creates trust. If you combine trust with responsibility, your subordinates will begin investing more of their own ingenuity into their job. Their productivity and the quality of their work will improve dramatically, which won't hurt your promotional efforts.

Be decisive, clear, and up front. All exceptional leaders have a clear vision of their goals. They are not afraid to make decisions to achieve their goals. Believing that honesty is the best policy, they tell it like it is even if it's not in their own best interest.

Encourage competition. Although outstanding leaders always create a climate of trust and team spirit within their organizations, they'll also encourage disagreement to prevent what Irving Janis, author of the book *Groupthink* (Houghton Mifflin College, 1982), called "Groupthink." Janis found that outstanding leaders often remove themselves from important discussions and even intentionally played devil's advocate to stimulate more ideas by creating environments for open discussions and the sharing of different ideas.

Don't be a workaholic. A workaholic uses work as an excuse to escape from their personal life. They're always scurrying around to find something to keep them busy as they try to convince others that they are truly indispensable. Workaholics are driven by their fear of failure that's based on their own low self-esteem and as a result, they seldom get promoted, and will never become leaders. Exceptional leaders on the other hand, measure the results of what they do against what it costs as they constantly prioritize their personal and professional lives. They place a priority on their personal lives and are not workaholics.

Improve each day. An executive friend of mine was always trying to improve on his leadership techniques. He'd tell me, "David, I believe that I can get just a little bit better at my job every day if I continue to look for ways to improve." He continued his daily self-improvement program right up to the day he retired and as a result, was an outstanding leader. Some people give up when they say, "What's the use? I'll never get the job I want because I'm just not good enough." Everybody can get better at whatever they do if they work on getting just a little bit better each day.

Focus on results. Exceptional leaders do not expect others to do things their way. They're not interested in processes and procedures. They're only interested in results and whether or not goals are achieved.

Respect others' feelings. Exceptional leaders always remember that people's responses are based on their feelings. Although they may approach problems in a purely rational manner, they will consider the feelings of others to determine how to solve a problem. What may seem trivial to one person may be vitally important to another. Always take the feelings of people into consideration in everything you do.

Do not let distractions keep you from becoming an exceptional leader. A distraction is anything that keeps you from doing what you should be doing such as watching television, making unnecessary phone calls, or listening to mindless chatter. Exceptional leaders do not invest their time in trivial pursuits, but rather in quality activities that offer a reasonable assurance of a return on their investment of time. They understand the benefits of time management.

(?) *Help: The Great Little Book on Effective Leadership* (Career Press, 1997) by Brian Tracy was written for anyone who is interested in learning more about what it takes to become an effective leader.

Working for a Jerk

What do you do if you're working for a jerk? As much as you may think he's a miserable worm, I'll bet he'd be awfully nice to you if you were more proficient at making him happy and at helping him make his boss happy. The irony of the situation is that most bosses have nothing to gain by keeping you happy. You can't provide your boss with a raise or promote him to the position that he wants. Why then should your boss be good to you just because you're doing a good job? If all you have going for you is your good work, then getting ahead while working for a jerk is like climbing Mount Everest in your bare feet. It can't be done.

In some cases, your jerk boss may not want you to do too good of a job. They may consider you a threat rather than an asset if they think you're after their job. Even if your boss owns the business, the fact that you're doing an outstanding job may frighten him. He may feel that because you're so good, the competition may hire you away to compete against his business. Here are several options to consider if you're working for a boss that's a real jerk:

Do nothing. Many people with problem bosses elect to do nothing because the thought of doing something makes them nervous. They're concerned about what will happen if their attempt to do something fails. Doing nothing is usually not a very good strategy unless you have a good reason. Maybe the idiot is retiring next month or she's been transferred to another department. If you elect to do nothing, you are in effect putting your career and promotion on hold. A boss that doesn't care about you is not going to help get you promoted.

Accept your boss. You may think you're working for a jerk when all you really have is a boss with a personality or management style that's different from yours. If he treats everybody the same way he treats you, it shouldn't become a personal issue with you. In this case, it may be easier for you to accept the situation for what it is and get on with your professional life.

Change yourself. Sometimes the best way to deal with a jerk is to not try to change them, but to change yourself. It's a lot easier to change yourself than to change someone else whom you have little or no control over. Think about what you can do to improve the situation. For example, if you're dealing with a boss who tries to bite your head off in front of everybody whenever you suggest an idea, try approaching him in private the next time you have an idea. If he still reacts the same way and you can't reconcile the situation, don't present him with any more new ideas. It may also be time to find a new boss.

Hold a one-on-one meeting. There's no sense in beating around the bush. Why not hold a one-on-one meeting with your boss and find out from the "horse's mouth" exactly what's going on. Obviously, you want to be as diplomatic as you can if you choose to use this approach. One of the ways to diffuse the situation is to put the onus on yourself. For example, you might say, "Boss, I have apparently done something to offend you but I don't know what it is. You shoot down every idea I present to you. Could you help me out and tell me what I'm doing wrong?"

In the final analysis, you must be able to either resolve the problems you're having with your boss or find a new boss who can ultimately help you get promoted. If you like the company and don't want to leave, look for transfer opportunities. Start developing an internal network of contacts that can help you find opportunities. If there are no viable transfer opportunities, then you may have to find another company.

(?) *Help:* How to Manage Your Boss (Career Press, 1994) by Dr. Roger Fritz and Kristie Kennard cover a variety of ways to cope with problem bosses. If you're working for a jerk, check out Robert Hochheiser's book, *How to Work for a Jerk.* The title says it all! Also check out *Jerks At Work* (Career Press, 1999) by Ken Lloyd.

Warning: Job-related stress is a well-known aspect of the business world. Psychologists place the blame on the fact that U.S. workers have been forced to make behavioral adjustment to a faster pace of change in today's dynamic corporate atmosphere. Although some people are aware of the harmful effects of stress, few know how to control or prevent it. Victimized by the stressful world they live in, many people have accepted stress as a necessary component of their job. However, there is a relatively simple way for you to alleviate stress and thus control its undesirable effects of eventually causing a heart attack. Relaxation will counteract the physiological effects of stress and it can be elicited by a simple mental technique to periodically think about something you like to do, such as fishing or golf.

Controlling Back Stabbers

Conflicts within an organization are like the body's temperature. As long as the temperature is still warm, the body is still alive, and presumably functioning. Conflict is a sign that the organization is alive and that people are doing what they are supposed to be doing, fighting with each other to arrive at the best possible solutions to problems. However, conflict between peers can be a royal pain in the backside, especially when the infighting involves a personal challenge to your level of competency or management ability.

It's difficult to try to excel at work if you're convinced that the deck is stacked against you because a peer constantly degrades you. The advancement of your career will unfortunately be hindered until the situation is rectified to your satisfaction. If you find yourself in this situation, cheer up. All is not lost if your back stabber is willing to meet with you privately to explain why they believe they have a charter to degrade you behind your back. You must confront them face-to-face to resolve the problem.

At the outset of the meeting, explain to them in very precise terms, the fact that you are aware of the condescending comments they're making about you. Then ask them, "Why are you doing this?" Listen very carefully to what they have to say. Most back stabbers are very insecure people and like to talk about others as their mechanism to get attention. The fact that you have caught them in the act should prove to be an embarrassment to them. The fact that you have confronted them may be enough to get them to stop talking about you and find another victim to ridicule.

If you confront a back stabber and they deny any wrongdoing, be prepared to divulge your sources of information. If they continue to deny your accusation, ask them to meet with you and one of your sources for a confrontation to get at the truth.

Although most back stabbers will not agree to such a meeting because they are basically cowards, it may shake them up enough to offer you a confession. At a minimum, they should stop degrading you for fear of another confrontation. End the meeting with a warning to reinforce your position. Let them know that if they continue to make illicit comments about you, you will take the matter up with their boss.

Whatever its cause, internal conflicts consume valuable time, drain energy, and are universally disliked throughout any organization. Avoid them like the plague. If the person who is ultimately responsible for your promotion becomes aware of the conflict, they may simply conclude that you are not worth the risk in the new position.

? *Help: Take Yourself to the Top* (Warner Books, 1998) by Laura Fortgang, one of the top career coaches in the country, not only talks about how to advance your career by using your network, but offers plenty of philosophical advice as well.

● *Warning:* Adverse human relations in the workplace catch everybody's eye because of their volatile status. Your challenge, when adversity raises its ugly head, is to neutralize the situation as quickly and painlessly as you can for obvious reasons. Any confrontation at any level that is directed at you is not conducive to your promotion objectives. I don't care if you are 1,000 percent right and your adversary is totally wrong, the situation will not help get you promoted.

Working for an Incompetent Boss

No discussion about incompetent bosses would be complete without first mentioning Dr. Laurence Peter and Raymond Hull's 1969 book, *The Peter Principle* (Buccaneer Books, 1969), that caused a major cultural phenomenon. Who can ever forget Dr. Peter's classic words, "In a hierarchy, every employee tends to rise to his or her level of incompetence." Applying this principle to incompetent bosses—nothing fails like success—is precisely what happens when competent employees are promoted into management. Competent people show high promotional potential in the lower ranks, but eventually reveal their incompetence when they become leaders. A recent survey of business failures showed that more than 50 percent of the failures were because of management incompetence. If you're working for an incompetent boss, here is how to control the various types of incompetents:

Wimps. Wimps are managers who are afraid to do anything and they will avoid initiating any action to help get you promoted probably because of their concern about finding your replacement. They are gutless wonders who refuse to take any risk whatsoever. Wimps are also classical compromisers who do things strictly by the book and will ponder ad infinitum over making the most trivial decision. They'll always maintain a stockpile of alibis and fall guys that they can use to cover their tracks. Wimps love to call meetings, form committees, participate on fact-finding studies, and hire outside consultants. They're experts at using diversionary tactics to hide problems. Over time, most wimps fizzle out in the power game because of their inaction. It's not uncommon for them to step out of management and back into the line organization if they are given the opportunity. How do you make a decision on your behalf that they refuse to make? Ask them if you can solicit the approval of their boss to take the heat off them. They'll probably tell you, "Yeah, if my boss says it's okay, then it is alright by me."

Screw-ups. Any manager is capable of making mistakes on occasion, but screw-ups make screwing up a way of life. They have neither the guts nor the brains to do anything right and have a difficult time managing their own career or any assignment given to them, let alone helping you progress on your own career path. Unfortunately, in spite of their gross incompetence, they do creep into upper management positions either because their father or father-in-law owns the business or some other screw-up promoted them so they'd have company at the top. If you are unfortunate to work for a screw-up, the value of any referral they can give you is highly questionable. Continue working for them if you believe they're going to be replaced in the near future or if you want their job. There is a good chance that they won't last very long.

Haters. Working for a boss who doesn't like you reduces your effectiveness to work for them. They will show their dislike by blocking your initiatives and thwarting your ambitions. What do you do? First, try and figure out a way to get your boss to start liking you. Find out what they dislike about you and correct the situation if possible. If you can't do that, there is no way he or she is ever going to help get you promoted so it may be time to find another boss.

No-ops. A particularly despicable type of managers is the no-op, that numskull who is always promising to do something for you and never does it. What do you do about it if you're working for a no-op manager who is totally incapable of making any kind of decision? The first thing you have to realize is that they will never help you get promoted on their own. If their boss tells them they want you to take over a new assignment, they'll accept the decision because they didn't have to make the decision. You can continue working for a no-op as long as their influence on your promotion is insignificant.

Bureaucrats. Bureaucrats love to say that although they agree with what you want to do, the organization's rules and regulations will not allow it. Incapable of independent thought, bureaucrats are often found in the roots of the management world. They thrive in old, established companies that are riddled with volumes of policies and procedures. Whenever bureaucrats feel threatened or endangered, they'll take refuge behind policies, official directives, a memorandum from a higher level, or any other document that allows them to stop an action. What do you do? If you can tolerate working for a bureaucrat, most of them will support your promotion because that is the bureaucratic way. Everybody is expected to move up the corporate ladder.

Micro-managers. Micro-managers are interested in knowing everything you're doing relative to your current job. Because they are micro-thinkers, they are only interested in short-term objectives and have no interest in your long-term objectives, like your promotional ambitions. If you work for one, you will find it difficult to get them to focus on any of your long-term goals. Although they won't stand in your way if you have an opportunity to get promoted, they won't offer you much help either. They are not well-versed in operating or thinking in a long-term environment, so if you have long-term promotional objectives, don't expect much help from a micro-manager. If you have short-term objectives, they can help you.

Macro-managers. In contrast, there is the macro-manager who is only interested in the big picture. They want to know what's going on in the entire organization and are only interested in its aggregate output measured in bottom line terms. You often hear macro-managers huff and puff at meetings when they stand up and declare that they are only interested in the big picture. They have blatantly little interest in details that point to the big picture, a quality that often gets them into trouble. They love long-term planning exercises so if your career objectives are long-term, they can help you put together an effective plan.

Regardless of the type of incompetent manager you may be working for, you've got to reconcile the situation if you want to keep your career on track. Although your boss may not care about your job satisfaction, you may be able to gain some insight about what's going on by catching him off guard, appealing to his ego by telling him you respect his advice, and asking him to share with you ideas on how you could get more out of your job. Tell him you're looking for opportunities to move up in the organization, earn more money, and do more fulfilling work. Avoid making any demand and don't give him the impression that you'll quit if you don't get what you want. If the response you get is totally negative and provides you with no constructive ideas, then you have at least qualified the situation. It's time to find another boss.

Warning: Have you ever taken a good look at the people you used to know who got promoted into lofty upper management positions? When they were colleagues, they were reachable and approachable, but when they moved up the corporate ladder, they became insufferable managers unable to delegate or communicate. Why? What happens that turns people into uncontrollable idiots when they assume positions of authority? Disastrous as they may seem at fulfilling all of the basic business functions like achieving productivity, profitability, and efficiency, most of them are still experts at getting and keeping more pay than the rest of us. They know how to use their power to get people working to meet their personal aims and the aims of their immediate organizations. So, before you conclude that the upper manager you need to get at to achieve your promotional objectives is a complete jerk, think again. He's got the title, the power, and the big salary that you don't have, so he can't be a complete jerk. Just maybe he has more on the ball than you give him credit for.

Handling Executive Encounters

It's not uncommon for an executive to approach you and ask for an informal presentation on a subject that they think you know something about. In most instances, they'll have first informed your boss of their request. One-on-one executive encounters offer you an opportunity to demonstrate how you are in a subject that's of interest to an executive who could influence your promotion. However, even if you are the world's foremost noted expert on the subject that is of interest to them, if you are not able to present the desired information in a format that motivates them, you will not accumulate any career points. In fact, you could even lose points if you fail to apply the appropriate motivational techniques in your one-on-one presentation. Here's what you need to keep in mind when you respond to one-on-one executive encounters:

First impression. The first 30-second impression an exec develops about you will be based on what you say, your facial expression, movement, and the tone of your voice. If that picture is positive, you have a chance to make an immediate and favorable impression. If the impression is negative, your odds are significantly reduced and you probably won't get a second chance. If an exec tells you politely that she will digest what you have said and will get back with you later, you can rest assured that you have not made a favorable impression.

Appearance. Your appearance is an important factor in one-on-one executive encounters. Your appearance can influence an exec's perception of you and may even determine their attitude toward you at the outset of your meeting with them. That's why people whose appearance suggests high status are treated measurably better than whose appearance suggest low status. Like it or not, that is a fact of life and most executives think of themselves as being in the upper echelon.

Body language. Nonverbal appearance, facial expressions, and what you say are an important part of one-on-one encounters. The exec must believe in their mind that you are a person who is committed to the company and loyal to the cause before they'll believe anything you tell them. Nonverbal communication from facial expression to body movement will be used to judge your initial worth. It tends to be even more heavily relied upon if your words give a contradictory message because it's one of the most revealing differences between powerful people and those with little power. You want to come across as a powerful person.

Strategic meetings with key people are one of the most powerful political tools you have in your promotional arsenal. Here's an example of how you can initiate an encounter with a key exec. Suppose you have a brilliant idea that when implemented, will catapult your company into Fortune 500 heaven. You know you're the best person in the world to successfully carry your idea off and there is only one executive who has the authority to approve your idea. How do you strategically meet with this person and motivate her to approve your idea?

Let's suppose you are at the company's party to celebrate the closure of its fiscal year with record high sales and earnings. It presents the perfect opportunity for you to rub elbows with Haley Williams, the division's new president. You have heard through a reliable grapevine that she has already started to scout for a senior vice president. Why not see if you can get a chance to step up to the plate and hit a home run? To take advantage of this situation, simply walk up to Haley, introduce yourself, and enter into a conversation that will leave her with a lasting favorable impression of you.

(?) *Help:* Suzette Elgin, in her book *BusinessSpeak* (McGraw-Hill, 1995), offers some excellent advice on how to use the gentle art of verbal persuasion to get what you want.

Maneuvering Through Group Encounters

If you're standing in front of a group of executives about to make a presentation, it is absolutely critical that the first minute of your presentation be viewed as positive rather than negative. The more you know about the culture and personality types of each exec in the group, the more accurately you can determine how to tailor your presentation to leverage a favorable first and lasting impression. Although I recognize that it is highly unlikely that all the execs in the group will have the same personality type, determining their personalities in advance of the meeting to gauge how you will want to structure your presentation is absolutely critical to your success.

Suppose you're walking down the hallway past the boardroom, and you're startled when the door suddenly opens. Your boss, Jerry, suddenly appears in front of you and says, "Quick, get in here and tell the board of directors everything you know about the Peabody Project. They think we're out of control and my backside is on the line if you don't convince them otherwise." Before you can utter a response, Jerry grabs you by the arm and you're suddenly standing at the head of the conference table facing a crowd of 12 board members. As Jerry introduces you to the board, you quickly survey the group to help determine how you will conduct your presentation. Here are several hints that will help you get started:

Grab their attention. To grab the attention of the group, show them the big picture of the project at the very outset of your presentation. Because you haven't had time to prepare any briefing charts, make use of the white board to quickly recap key project status points. For example, you may want to compare project cost to actual cost, noting the reasons for any over or under runs.

Be consistent. Remember, the more consistent you can make what you say with how you say it, the more favorable your first impression will be. Consistency covers the use of all three channels of communication including body language, voice, and words. If you're presenting important figures and smiling at the same time, you're not consistent in emphasizing the importance of the message you're trying to convey. A more serious look is in order for serious presentations. Always know what your face is saying. It's your most controllable nonverbal clue and the one the execs will be relying on to gauge your attitude.

Look them in the eye. Gesture with purpose and always toward your execs. Don't make cramped gestures or quick movements and never fiddle with coins, bracelets, a pen, ties, or other objects to distract them during your presentation.

Smiling and head nodding are the most powerful non-verbal clues you can use when addressing execs. Start your presentation off with direct eye contact as your point of reference and adjust from there. If you are uncomfortable about making eye contact, look at the person's forehead. Unless they are very close to you, they will not be able to tell you are avoiding direct eye contact.

Dealing With Firefighters

"Firefighters" thrive in crisis environments. They're never content to have things under control and are always on the lookout for a new catastrophe. If none exist, they'll find an assortment of insignificant problems and blow them up to colossal proportions so that they can marshal their forces to prevent whatever disaster they predict will happen if no action is taken.

Firefighters have no sense of business politics and do not know how to set priorities. As a result, they are very demanding on their people and expect them to be as driven as they are by any perceived crisis. They often drive the people who work for them crazy by perpetually changing what they want done and are constantly dreaming up new crisis projects. Firefighter managers are disasters at administrating or planning anything. They'll stop at nothing to meet a crisis objective and because they do everything in extremes, if they make a mistake, it can be a whopper!

Firefighters tend to be power addicts because of their need to feed off power. The more power they can get, the more they want. Single-minded and egomaniacal, they don't care about the growth of anything other than their own personal empires. Driven to control everything and everyone in sight, they must have the last word and be the final authority on any subject, no matter how minor. They are more interested in bossing people around than they are in getting anything done. If you stand in their way, they will use all of their energies to get rid of you, even if you are right and they are wrong. So, do not ever stand in their way or even think about soliciting their help to get you promoted. They won't do it because of their perception that anyone who leaves their organization drains their power base.

Lots of firefighters are also con artists. They're the politicians of the corporate world. If they can't achieve what they want with brute force, they will resort to finesse and lies to accomplish what they want. These are the bosses who promise you everything and deliver nothing but tidbits of information and more promises. They like to give you company T-shirts, take you out to lunch, and send you one-liner e-mail messages telling you how good you are. Good con artists and firefighters will put their arms around you, tell you how far you'll get by following their instructions, while they pick your pocket with the other hand and your brain with conversation. No matter how much they say they like your work, they'll tell their boss your mistakes are the cause of their problems if it suits their needs.

Regardless of what type of firefighter you may be dealing with, they are all troublesome. They have no interest in your ambitions for promotion and in fact, they can hurt you promotional efforts if they believe that it will serve their personal cause. If you are unfortunately working for a firefighter, what can you do? Short of finding a better boss to work for, there is not much that you can do to change the situation. Maintain a low profile, appeal to their egos, and hope that they will soon be replaced.

(?) *Help: Thriving in Chaos* (Alfred A. Knopf Press, 1987) by Tom Peters talks about the unique opportunities that can be found in chaotic business environments when everyone else is running for cover.

Managing Conflicts

Conflicts result when a disagreement, a controversy, or a personal clash occurs between two or more people. The word itself connotes something serious, and for this reason, should be avoided as much as possible. As everybody knows from experience, conflicts are unpleasant, they're disruptive to relationships, are counterproductive, and can be costly to your promotional efforts. Nobody walks away from a conflict situation as an absolute winner. Unfortunately, conflicts are an inevitable part of human relationships. Here's what you do to minimize your exposure to conflicts and how to control conflicts so that they will have a minimal disruptive effect on your promotional efforts:

The listening approach. Often, a few minutes of listening to a person can do wonders to diffuse a potential conflict situation. Even if you disagree with the person, allow them to get their feelings out into the open where they can at least be addressed to hopefully resolve the conflict. Resolve as many conflicts as you can on the spot.

The controlled approach. A confrontation starts with words that directly point at the person who is being confronted. Words like "You did this..." or "You're the one who is responsible for..." will generally trigger a hot confrontation that can quickly escalate into a conflict. If someone approaches you with confrontational words, you can often diffuse the situation with counter words like "I'm sorry you feel that way. Can we discuss it?" or "Although I respect your opinion, we need to review...." If the confrontation occurs in the presence of other people, do everything you can to control your temper. Invite the person to meet with you privately in your office to discuss whatever is bothering them. If they refuse your offer and continue with their confrontation, you are better off walking away from the situation than engaging them in a confrontation that can be witnessed by other people.

The "I win, you lose" approach. This conflict situation usually occurs when there is a confrontation between a subordinate and a superior. In its simplest form, a subordinate approaches a superior and says, "I want to do the following...." The superior says, "No, you can't do that" and the conflict is over. The superior wins and the subordinate loses. But did you really win? You've built up some animosity with your subordinate that could come back to haunt you later. Always offer an explanation to help minimize a "no" response in a confrontation. If a person understands why you said no, even if they don't agree with your reason, they are more likely to accept your answer.

The no-lose approach. The alternative to the win-lose approach is the no-lose approach. The no-lose method is an open-ended approach to conflict resolution where neither party involved in the conflict knows for sure what the solution will be since it's left open. You can initiate a no-lose approach by making a statement like, "Let's put our heads together and see if we can come up with a solution that meets both our needs." The downside of this method is that it involves trade-offs that both parties must be willing to make. The upside is that the approach facilitates the use of cooperation to effectively eliminate what could have been a conflict.

Some people believe that they need to exercise their power to increase their influence over others to demonstrate their worth for a higher position in the organization. They quickly forget their own negative experiences when people used power over them. The more you use power to manipulate subordinates, the less influence you will have over anybody, and the less chance you will have at getting yourself promoted.

? *Help:* *Business Etiquette* (Career Press, 1997) by Ann Marie Sabath offers concise, engaging solutions to business etiquette dilemmas in conflicting situations.

Welcome All New Ideas

James is the former CEO of a medium-size manufacturing company who's spending his retirement years in bitterness. I first met James in his spectacular executive office when he was CEO and he struck me as a pompous man who reveled in being a big frog in a small pond. I arrived at his office a few minutes before our appointment and started rummaging through the company's magazine when I noticed that he was prominently featured in the magazine's lead article.

The article described him in almost messianic terms and praised his management style. According to the article, his keen incisiveness, gruff exterior, and bluntness marked his "excellent" management style. I learned from the article that one of his favorite gambits when anyone presented him with a new idea was to say, "Are you ready for a grilling on your idea?" A few minutes later when I met with him to review my proposal, he used those exact words: "Are you ready for your grilling?"

I have always believed that a potentially good idea can't come about unless it is discussed openly. Moreover, if the discussion is to work, it has to be done in an objective environment. My objection in dealing with James stemmed from the fact that he took such glee in conducting a grilling rather than objectively discussing the merits or lack of merits in any idea presented to him. As a result of the grilling he gave me, he never heard any of my good ideas, because the communications was all one-way, with James acting as both judge and juror. I believe he enjoyed the fact that everyone who approached him did so in a state of terror. I later found out why he had retired in bitterness. Unbenounced to him, his entire executive staff met privately with the board of directors and demanded his resignation. Their request was honored that same day.

Idea: *Forbes* magazine's annual corporate survey last year showed that 90 percent of the companies admitted that their management training programs left a lot to be desired. One of the exceptions was Tassani Communications who encourages managers to spend time with other managers on a recurring basis. Managers are given the option of selecting a peer manager to shadow or the group's executive picks one for them. In either event, their objective is to follow a peer around for a day and learn what they do to broaden their own perspective. As Tassani's vice president put it, "It's a great way to get everybody in the company involved in training, it doesn't cost a lot of money for the program, and it encourages support between managers." Your ability to solicit support from peers is a favorable quality that upper management looks for when they consider anybody for a promotion.

Know How To Say Yes

Making a decision always puts the decision-maker in a vulnerable position. That's because a "yes" decision tags the decision-maker with taking the initiative and allows onlookers to pass judgment on the quality of the decision. As a result, it becomes human nature to avoid making a decision in the hopes that tough issues will somehow resolve themselves. Unfortunately, this seldom happens and the non-decision-makers end up getting clobbered by the onlookers anyway for not making a decision.

The "yes" decision usually carries more risk than the "no" decision because it demands that something gets implemented. As we all know, things can go wrong during the implementation stage. Even if the "yes" decision was the right initial decision, the decision-maker still gets blamed if things go wrong during implementation. So why not play it safe and only make "no" decisions?

Saying no in order to play it safe doesn't reduce one's vulnerability of being cited for failure if you had said yes. In the past, you might have been able to skate up the corporate ladder with this kind of thinking. That was when the return-on-asset philosophy dominated the decision-making thought process of many executives who were unwilling to say yes on long-term ventures that were critical to their company's survival.

Every company that has grown to any stature has done so because the founders committed overwhelmingly to affirmative ideas. They believed against all odds that their products and services would survive if they said yes to well-thought-out ideas. If your company has lost touch with the "yes" word, it is in trouble or soon will be. If you don't know how to say yes, you're in trouble. Yes means commitment. Making the commitment demands the commitment of time, effort, people, and money. It's at the heart of all our great corporations. It's what you get paid to do the higher up the corporate ladder you move. If you are not willing to make "yes" decisions, then you can kiss your promotional ambition goodbye.

Idea: Write down five key decisions you have made over the past year. Which ones were "yes" decisions? If it's less than three, you're likely avoiding making "yes" decisions. What key decisions are you now facing? Which ones deserve a "yes" decision?

Take the Heat

I once served on a search committee for a nonprofit association that was desperately looking for an executive director to replace the one who had retired after serving for 25 distinguished years. The board of directors knew it would be difficult to find a comparable replacement and asked me to participate because of my experience in searching for similar positions. The search ended up taking longer than anyone had expected. After six months, we were still looking for the perfect candidate. The position was considered an attractive opportunity and we were subsequently flooded with resumes. We met for several hours every two weeks to interview candidates and to discuss qualified applicants.

Eventually, five candidates emerged with one appearing to be the front runner. The sentiments of everyone on the committee but me were with the front runner because of his track record and strong recommendations from respected professionals in the association. A lot can be told from the way a person writes their resume and responds to pointed questions during an interview. I didn't like the excessive vanity in his resume or the way he avoided eye contact when I asked him difficult questions during the interview.

Initially, I kept quiet about my reservations with the hopes that the lead candidate would stumble without any intervention from me. The field was finally reduced to two candidates that included the lead candidate who had done nothing to sway my initial opinion of him. That's when I broke the ice and stunned the committee members when I told them their first choice candidate was, in my opinion, flawed. I can assure you I took more heat than French fries do at McDonald's when I made that statement.

Follow-up meetings with both candidates were scheduled and fortunately, the charm and charisma of the front-runner faded when he was put to the test. The second-place candidate was offered the position and she's still with the association doing an outstanding job today. Membership is up and the association's programs have expanded dramatically.

When I first voiced my views about the front runner, I ruffled everybody's feathers. After the follow-up interview, I made some allies. By the time the search was over, everybody on the search committee was my friend for life. I'm glad I took the heat. When the time is right, and you've examined the evidence, take a stand and be willing to go against the grain. That's the mark of a true leader. Your courage won't go unnoticed by those who are responsible for your promotion.

Manage Failure

Failure is one of the most powerful words in the English language. The mere sound of the word is enough to slam you against the wall. Whenever we engage in an important activity that ends in failure, we often recoil from it and try to disassociate ourselves from the failure. Being identified with failure is often so offensive that people will blame their failures on anything. If you make it a practice of letting yourself off the hook for something you were responsible for, you make it that much easier to make the same error again.

Who can deny how easy it is to adopt the "they did it" mentality. When you do that, you invite a repeat of the failure you're attempting to avoid. How often have you heard the excuse, "It was due to a computer error" or "They didn't listen to my advice." This human attribute often leads us down the path of self-deception and prevents us from learning from our mistakes or even making decisions. You risk becoming like the man who never made a mistake because he never made a decision.

Part of our difficulty in accepting failure is our refusal to see its positive aspects. In our innate desire to put as much distance between failure and ourselves as we can, we obliterate any opportunity to have it contribute to our confidence. You have to wrestle with failure all the way down to the ground before you can get hold of it. If you don't run from it, you'll eventually be able to control it rather than having it control you. Anytime you fail, treat it like a challenge and perform a full autopsy to learn from your mistakes. In the process, you'll learn how to make higher stake decisions in the future with a greater probability of success.

If you can't learn to live and learn from your failures, you'll severely handicap your opportunities for promotions. Think of a mistake you've recently made but avoided acknowledging. Tell yourself, "I failed" 20 times or until it sinks into your thinking. Wrestle that failure to the ground, pull out your knife, and dissect it. How did it occur and what did you learn from it? Once you learn how to own your mistakes, you'll quickly discover how the world doesn't come to an abrupt end because of your failures and you can get on with the task of promoting yourself.

Embrace Change

A highly regarded systems engineer at Hewlett Packard told me, "I feel threatened. The life cycle of a product around here is less than six months and if I can't keep up with the pace, I'll be a veritable antique before I reach 30." Today's skills, knowledge, and products live fast and die young. We are all being asked to learn on the fly and produce more with less money at a laser fast pace that will continue to accelerate. "Change is happening faster than we can keep tabs on it and change threatens to shake the foundations of America's most secure corporations," warned a recent study by the U.S. Congress's Office of Technology. No industry will escape it and no one is exempt. Your ability to accept change and adjust to it will be mandatory if you want to get yourself promoted.

In the face of accelerating change in every area of our lives, the conventional thinking that guided us in the past is outdated today. A vivid example of what happens when you stick with conventional wisdom occurred in the early days of football. In 1905, football was a low scoring sport of running and kicking the ball. A bunch of guys in leather helmets would line up and see if they could push the other team back for a three- or four-yard gain. A four-yard gain was a big deal.

When the forward pass was legalized in 1906, it was suddenly possible to gain 40 or more yards with the flick of a wrist. During the first season, most of the teams stayed with their conventional running games. Recognizing that football had entered a new era in which the three-yard strategy was obsolete, the coaches at St. Louis University adapted quickly, and switched to a forward passing offensive game. That season, they outscored their opponents 402 to 11!

Each day, we face changes that are as challenging as the adoption of the forward pass was to football. Every time we turn around, the rules of the game have changed. You can no longer afford to recycle, modify, or revise the conventional wisdom of the past. The pace of the changes in the new millennium will make the 1990s look like a walk in the park. Tim Nelsen, an enlightened friend of mine told me, "The time to change is when you don't have to, when you're on the crest of the wave, not when you're in the trough." (He and I used to surf at Santa Cruz, California when we were in college.)

In an environment where waves of change are coming at us from all directions, Tim's metaphor was right on. Keep changing while you are ahead of the wave by initiating action that's required to make the change happen in your organization. Don't get caught in the trap of just paying lip service to change, or you'll never catch the wave. You'll be just another observer standing on the beach watching all of the action that's taking place out in the surf. And beachcombers are not the ones who get promoted. The future belongs to those who know how to make change happen before anyone else even knows what's going on.

Terminate Terminators

A terminator is any person who, for whatever reason, wants to get you terminated from your job. If a terminator ever confronts you, you can kiss your promotional dreams goodbye if you don't handle the situation right. Make no mistake about it, everybody will face several terminators during the course of their careers. If you've been targeted by a terminator, they will use their aggressive behavior and all of the influence they can muster to either shove you back or get you fired.

Several years ago, I was working for a senior vice president who was a total idiot.

Needless to say, it took just five months for the CEO to discover what I already knew, and he fired this guy much to my relief. The

CEO brought in a replacement vice president fresh from the ranks of a growing division. I'll never forget the introductory meeting that took place in the boardroom. In walks the new vice president (Steve), a short squat man with a nepoleonic stature and his protege, a young kid (Mike) who I swear was throwing rose pedals out in front of Steve as he walked up to the podium to tell us about all of his great accomplishments.

Steve made it clear to all of us that his way was the only way of doing things.

He introduced Mike as his right-hand man who would assist him in implementing his programs. Mike was Steve's appointed terminator. It was clear to me at the time that our CEO, in his infinite wisdom, had selected another idiot vice president who wouldn't last long. It was also clear to me that this guy and his terminator represented a threat to my promotional ambitions. In the interest of survival, let me share with you my survival plan:

When confronted by a terminator: Hold your ground and do not change your position. If you don't do this, it is a sign of weakness that terminators look for, and like a vampire, they'll move in for the kill. Don't go on the defensive or the offensive. State your positions in clear terms that anyone can understand, and stare into the eyes of your would-be terminator. If he counters your position with another position, say nothing unless you are asked for an opinion. If a terminator asks you what you think about their position, simply say, "You're certainly entitled to your opinion." It is very difficult for terminators to effectively respond when they are confronted on equal grounds.

When under attack by a terminator. If given the chance, an aggressive terminator will jump in and attack you with both barrels. You're in a meeting, making an important presentation when they jump into the middle of a sentence and tell everybody within shouting distance, "That'll never work." Don't try to overpower an attacking terminator, and whatever you do, control your anger. Let the terminator's anger flow into the audience when you tell him,

"Mike, why don't you listen to the rest of my presentation before you make any final judgments."

Neutralize their position. One of the best ways to neutralize a terminator is to play on their domineering egos. Suppose you're making a presentation. At the conclusion of your presentation, you say, "Mike has several ideas that he would like to share with you regarding the contents of my presentation." Look what you have accomplished in that simple statement. You have openly announced that you are a team player and that you value Mike's opinion, even if you really don't. If he stands up and starts lambasting everything you have said, he casts himself into the position of an outcast.

Strike for peace. Whenever you're confronted by a terminator, you are on the defensive, whether you like it or not. Always remember that the terminator has the perceived authority to eliminate your position. Even if they don't have the authority, they can do irreparable harm to your career, so never close the door in their face if you can avoid it. Even if their attacks on you are unfounded, leave the door open so that they will have room to back off. If you can reach a peaceful settlement with a terminator, you win. Over time, if they discover that you are too hard a nut to crack, they'll move onto another potential victim and leave you alone.

If you are someone who is not used to playing the role of a diplomat or negotiator, get used to it when you confront terminators. Playing these positions allows you to move in and out of confrontations with terminators without damaging their egos. It gives them a chance to see what you're made of as they take a measure of your character and commitment. Most of them are on an assignment to a higher level. If you can win their respect, they'll seek out someone else to terminate.

Idea: James Thurber, the great humorist, once said, "He who hesitates is sometimes saved. Most of the time, they'll lose." Be aggressive as you seek to find the high road to get yourself promoted. If anyone gets in your way, politely move them off to the side. If they refuse to move, go through them!

Shoot Snipers

As we all know, snipers hide in the dark alleys of the corporate world, and when you least expect it, they'll jump out and try to do anything they can to embarrass or humiliate you, making sarcastic comments about you to anyone who will listen. Most corporate snipers are chickens, so they'll only make their adverse comments behind your back when you're not around. However, if they're left unchecked, they tend to spawn others into becoming snipers to undermine your promotional ambitions.

A good friend of mine told me a classic story about a sniper and what she did to kill the problem. One week after Susan was promoted to director, she was walking down the hallway when she noticed Dan, one of her charges, standing by the water fountain talking to several of her employees. Everybody was laughing and having a good time as Dan waved his arms and proceeded to tell what she assumed was one heck of a joke. As Susan drew nearer to the group, the laughing suddenly stopped, and since Dan couldn't see her because he was facing the other way, she heard him say, "Yeah, this new director can't chew gum and think at the same time." The group quickly broke up when Susan innocently bent over to get a drink of water.

Susan told me, "If you ever have to deal with a sniper, you have got to eliminate their ability to hide what they're saying about you. Because their perceived power is derived from covert rather than overt actions, once you expose their position, their fear of retaliation will stop them dead in their tracks. You have to deal with them directly and assertively." Here's what Susan did:

Find them. In the example, Susan accidentally discovered when she approached the water fountain that Dan was a sniper. She was lucky because most snipers are very secretive about their exploits.

You may have to rely heavily on your network of friends and associates to uncover snipers. You can't take the offensive unless you know who the enemy is.

Confront them. The one fear that all snipers have is being confronted by the person they're sniping at. Remember, they are first-degree chickens. One of the best ways to confront one is to call them into you office, and with an innocent and neutral look on your face, ask them, "Why are you saying these things about me behind my back? Have I done something to offend you?" Then, sit back and wait for their response. If it take five minutes for them to muster the courage to give you a response, wait for it and say nothing. If they tell you, "It was just a joke," counter with another question like, "Why do you think it was funny?" Probing questions will virtually remove whatever is left of their spine.

Eliminate them. If a sniper starts to make more accusations when you confront them, you've got two basic choices to resolve the situation. First, is it worth your while to find out what you have done personally or professionally to cause their sniping? They may have a valid point that you were completely unaware of and you can take immediate action to correct the situation. If, on the other hand, their position is not valid, you may have to move to your second option and become the terminator. If the sniper is one of your direct reports, formally write them up for insubordination stating that they will be terminated if another instance occurs. If they are not a direct report, meet with their boss and apprise them of the situation. Be prepared to escalate the problem as high as you need to go to eliminate a sniper.

Sometimes, the problem with a sniper can be handled in a rational manner by taking the initiative to meet with them. Whenever possible, work with them to figure out what you can do to assure that it doesn't happen again. Now, you're showing the marks of a true leader. Tell your sniper "friend" that the next time he or she has a problem with you to bring it to your attention so that you have an opportunity to address the problem.

Watch Out for Know-it-Alls

The classic know-it-alls. You've seen them in action as they try to control people and events by dominating conversations with their impervious remarks. They will try to eliminate any opposition to their ideas by finding flaws and weaknesses to discredit others' points of view. Unfortunately, know-it-alls are generally very bright people and they are experts at making you look bad if it suits their needs. If you are confronted by a know-it-all, you have got to get them to open up their mind to new ideas and information, which is not a trivial task. Here are several ideas that'll help you overcome know-it-alls:

Know your facts. Proficient know-it-alls have excellent information filters that are built into their ears. If there are any flaws in the information you're using to make your point, their radar sensors will immediately pick up on them and they'll use your misinformation to discredit your ideas. Always check your information and sources first, before you present your ideas to a know-it-all. They have blatantly little patience, so make sure you present your ideas in clear, precise terms.

Stroke them. When you're dealing with a know-it-all, you must convince them that you have listened to and heard everything that they said. If you can convince them that you believe their ideas are brilliant, you'll stand a much better chance of getting them to listen and accept your ideas. Know-it-alls are experts at knowing when they are being conned because people try to con them all the time. When you stroke a know-it-all, make sure your demeanor shows respect and sincerity.

Blend with them. If you can convince a know-it-all that you truly appreciate their opinion and you want to incorporate their thoughts into the implementation of your own ideas, you have a good chance of hooking them for their support. For example, if they offer you one of their standard dismissals like, "We don't have time for this right now," dovetail their concern into your plan. Tell them,

"Although I agree with you that we don't have time, let's look at the consequences of what could happen it we don't act now."

Direct them. A subtle approach to get what you want out of a know-it-all is to direct their thought process. Be careful because if they figure out what you're doing, they'll slam the door in your face. You might first ask them what they think about the topic of your idea, and then state your idea in nonemotional tones. Logical follow-on statements to make that will help you direct a know-it-all down the path you want them to go would be, What if..., Maybe we could..., or With your help, we could....

If you can convince a know-it-all that you recognize and appreciate an expert when you see one, and tell them you believe they are one, you become less of a threat to them. The key is to get know-it-alls to spend their time working with you rather than against you. As your good ideas prove worthy after they are implemented, you'll impress the know-it-all and gain their respect. Just make sure you don't turn yourself into a know-it-all in the process.

Delegate Everything You Can

If you want to be truly effective at utilizing your time and expand your promotion possibilities at the same time, start delegating more of your work out to others. In his bestseller, *The Seven Habits of Highly Effective People*, leadership authority Steven Covey says, "Effective delegating to others is perhaps the single most powerful high-leverage activity there is." Time-management expert Harold Taylor says, "Delegation is the most important part of being a manager."

Today more than ever, the effective use of your time is critical to getting yourself promoted. How you use your time will determine what impact you'll have on your organization, and make no mistake about it, those who can promote you will be watching. There are several ways you can improve the use of you time: You can arrive at work early in the morning before anyone else so you can work without interruption. You can also prepare a detailed schedule of each day to maximize your use of time. Although these approaches will help improve your use of time, you are still the primary production resource. It's only when you delegate work to someone else that you become the secondary production resource.

One of the obvious benefits of delegating is that it saves you time. If you can successfully delegate some of your activities to others, it frees you up to work on the things that only you can do. Note that I used the word "successfully" as a qualifier in my last sentence. If you just dump some of your work off to someone else without doing the proper planning, you're wasting your time. If a person fails to complete important delegated tasks or makes serious mistakes, you could spend more time reconciling the situation than what you would have if you had done the task yourself. It could also damage your promotional options. Here are several guidelines to keep in mind when you delegate work:

State the desired results. When you delegate a task, explain the results you expect the person to achieve. Don't start by identifying the tasks required to do the work, which will limit the creativity of the person doing to work. Talk about the end results you expect.

Delegate in writing. When you and the other person agree on the goal of the delegated assignment, write it down. If you're using any performance standards to measure the quality of the job, identify the standards you will use and give a copy of the written agreement to the person doing the work.

Establish a timeline. Make sure you and the person doing the work agree on when the job will be done. If your timeline doesn't match with theirs, be flexible and agree upon a revised schedule. Allowing people to set their own timeline is far more preferable than forcing yours onto them. Agree on interim schedule reviews.

Grant authority. Whenever you assign work, you must give the person the power to act and to exercise their own initiatives. Make sure all the people who are affected by your delegated work know who you have delegated the work to.

Assign accountability. Always delegate a complete task, which heightens a person's interest and sense of accountability. Splitting a task between people fragments accountability and leaves you open to personal conflicts between people.

Get acceptance. Make sure the person responsible for the delegated task is in full agreement with what needs to be done, the schedules, and the expected results. You want more than murmured approval or tacit acceptance. You need an outright statement from the person that they agree to everything that's required in the delegated assignment.

Follow up. Give the person to whom you've delegated work breathing room to perform. It demonstrates your confidence in them. However, you must follow up to make sure delegated tasks are successfully completed. Set up weekly or monthly reviews so that you can assure yourself that delegated tasks are not getting away from you.

Warning: Never delegate assignments that your boss asked you to complete personally. Your boss may have a special reason for asking you to handle the assignment yourself. If you feel strongly that the assignment is appropriate to delegate, discuss it with your boss first.

Help: *The No-Lose Way to Release the Productive Potential of People* (Bantam Doubleday, 1986) by Dr. Thomas Gordon is an excellent book if you're interested in learning more about increasing productivity. Frank Huppe wrote *Successful Delegation* (Career Press, 1994), which is filled with great ideas on what it takes to become a successful delegater.

Play It Safe

In this day and age, everybody is emphasizing the importance of change. No matter how positive a change may be, most people will try to avoid or resist it secretly if they can get away with it. The fact that you're striving to get yourself promoted represents a change within your organization. If you get lulled into thinking that everybody will consider your promotion a positive change because of your delightful personality and management style, think again. They may smile when you meet them in the hallway and tell you how great it would be if you got promoted, but privately, they are singing a different song.

How will you handle the inevitable question you'll be asked when you interview for the position of your dreams: "What ideas do you have that will change the focus of this job and the direction of our organization?" Depending upon whom you're talking to, how you answer this question may well determine if you get the job. When it comes time to promote someone, the natural tendency of those who are responsible for making the decision will be to play it safe by sticking with someone they know. If they don't know you, you will not get the job. So what if you have great ideas that will bring lots of needed vitality to the new position? If they're fire-hosers, they are experts at undermining daring strategies and new ideas because they're not interested in changing anything. In the face of change, they will pull in the reigns, batten down the hatches, and play it safe.

Let's listen in on what someone who likes to play it safe might say about you to a colleague after your job interview. "Yeah, this guy sounds great. I can't believe all of the new ideas he wants to implement if he gets the job. Although I can't disagree with anything he wants to do, I am not sure we're ready for all those changes yet. Maybe next year. Let's go with the other candidate. She wants to maintain the status quo that we need right now." Boom! You didn't get promoted because you gave straight answers about your job ideas to someone who wasn't interested in changing. Be very careful as to how you answer interview questions. Taylor your answers so that they complement the personality of the person you're addressing. Here's how to handle interview questions from people with different business objectives:

Bottom-liners. In their dogged pursuit of the bottom line, bottom-liners have replaced creative thinking with myopic thinking. They're the Paul Reveres that are always running around on their high horses yelling, "Trim the fat, cut the costs, get lean and mean." Everything they see is in terms of numbers. New ideas are viewed by bottom-liners as potential problems that will extract profit from the bottom line, rather than pragmatic opportunities. If you're interviewing with a bottom-liner, only present your ideas that will have an immediate impact on the bottom line. Avoid addressing any long-term strategies because they will be meaningless to a short-term bottom-liner.

Seasoned veterans. God bless the seasoned veteran who has seen it all. They'll ask you a question and before you can even begin to respond, they'll give you the answer because they've seen it all. They believe that their vast experience will prevent any disaster from occurring even if they decide to hire you for the job. If you present them with an idea, they will quickly recall someone who failed miserably trying to implement a similar idea. You'll be blessed with the benefit of their experience when they explain why your idea won't work. Assuming that you are willing to work for this type of person, agree with anything they say during the interview.

Firehosers. Firehosers are the people who will at first agree with your ideas and then add their favorite word: *but!* "What a great idea, but it won't work. It's not in the budget and the CEO will never go for it. No one has ever done that before, but it is still a good idea. Let's discuss it at another time." Learn to recognize when you're being firehosed. Firehosers are not receptive to any major change, so don't suggest any. Instead, just tell them you plan to "fine tune" the existing organization.

Jewels. What happens if you're confronted by a decision-maker who legitimately wants to promote someone who'll bring a wealth of new ideas and vitality into the organization? Start off with your basic ideas and carefully listen to their responses to make sure you're not dealing with a firehoser in disguise. If they are truly a jewel, they will be receptive to your innovative ideas.

Always play it safe by knowing in advance something about the person who will be interviewing you. Ask around to find out what they like and dislike. What are their work habits and how do they think? The people who work for them are your best sources for this type of information.

? *Help: Think Like a Manager* (Career Press, 1993) by Roger Fritz tells you about everything they didn't tell you when you got promoted.

Chapter 9

Summary and Conclusions

Promoting yourself is a never-ending game and it's one of the toughest challenges you will ever face. By reading *1,001 Ways to Get Promoted*, you have kicked off your journey up the corporate ladder. Pay close attention to how you apply the promotional tenets. If you use them in harmony and balance, you will realize all of your promotional dreams. As you reach beyond where you are now on the corporate ladder, are you ready to take on the exciting challenges that accommodate your next promotion? Are you proficient at applying all of the tools offered in this book to help you get there?

As we enter into a new century, you can't help but wonder what it will be like working in 2005, 2010, and beyond. We all want to attain a higher quality of life. That's human nature. We saw a rapid change in the way people worked in the 1990s and it will continue to evolve as we close the 20th century. You'll be designing what you do by changing how things get done from the inside out to accommodate the dynamics that are flowing through our society and corporations at rip roaring speeds. For some of you, this will be a revolution. For others, it will be a natural evolution that you've already started.

Just in case you haven't noticed, we have also entered the age of entrepreneurialism. It's where our culture has been heading since the early 1990s. The age of entrepreneurialism is an age of experts. As you climb up the corporate ladder, it will be your job to find your niche and be the best you can be at filling that niche. Continue to develop your network along the way because the higher up in the food chain you go, the more you're going to need it. Your career successes will also depend upon how good of an entrepreneur you become.

To be successful in this entrepreneurial environment, you'll need to be very clear about who you are, what you can do, and what you want to do because you will literally be shaping your own career path. And as the director of your own career, you'll need to know where you fit in the overall scheme of things. As you evolve, you will recognize that there are things you do better than everybody else. And when you exploit your personal assets, people will take notice and promote you. There is no need to reinvent yourself. Just fine-tune what you already have to take advantage of your talents.

Work your strengths first and as you have time, work on improving your weak points. Nothing will be more important than how you design your work life so that it fits into the rest of your life. Don't make it a battle because it should be a natural progression. Have lots of fun in the process. The more you insist on making everything in your life right, the easier the transition will be. As you jump out of the box, there is no such thing as being afraid of consequences, of constant change, and of competition. Use the promotional tenets to help forge your way through the corporate jungle and continue to design your life without limits.

I wish you the very best of luck at having a successful career and a great life.

Certificate

If you would like to receive a beautiful parchment I've Been Promoted Certificate that's autographed by the author, just send a stamped self-addressed envelope to:

David Rye
c/o Western Publications
7741 N. Via Camello Del Sur
Scottsdale, Arizona 85258

Index